America's Great Delis
Recipes and Traditions from Coast to Coast

By Sheryll Bellman

SELLERS
PUBLISHING

For Nani and
Gagu and all our
grandmothers,
who, through their
love of food, have
instilled sweet
food memories
in us all.

Published by Sellers Publishing, Inc.
Copyright © 2010 Sheryll Bellman

Sellers Publishing, Inc.
161 John Roberts Road, South Portland, Maine 04106
For ordering information:
(800) 625-3386 toll free
Visit our Web site: www.sellerspublishing.com • E-mail: rsp@rsvp.com

First published in 2005 by Collectors Press, Inc.

ISBN: 13: 978-1-4162-0565-4
Library of Congress Control Number: 2009934665

Cover design by George Corsillo/Design Monsters

Printed and bound in China.

PROVERB:

No Festival
without a Feast

The Talmud

Contents

FROM A PEDDLER'S CART
TO A CULTURAL TRADITION
Introduction

Postcard, circa 1900. *(Courtesy of Rabbi Peter Schweitzer)*

The delicatessen, or deli, is a piece of modern Jewish history. The delis of yesterday contain more than pastrami sandwiches and cheese blintzes. Historically, delis feed a hunger for American Jews that goes way beyond the stomach. They offer the sense of identity and the feeling of being "home."

Between 1881 and 1924 two million Jewish people immigrated to the United States from Eastern Europe, and three-quarters of them settled in New York City. By 1910 they had become the largest single immigrant group in the city. It is the cuisine of the Ashkenazim that we most often think of as delicatessen food — matzo ball soup, noodle kugel, gefilte fish, potato latkes.

German and Alsatian immigrants were the first to open and run delicatessens in this country. Jewish immigrants soon followed. Today, many of the delis still operating are run by third- and fourth-generation family members. There is a pride in what they do and in what they offer, and a love for the life they have inherited.

The Jewish deli is more than a place that sells food; its heritage is of a gathering place where displaced people could find community. The newly arrived immigrants had much to endure, including severely cramped living conditions. Because of those living conditions, people spilled out into the streets, which became the focus of their daily life. By 1900 more than 25,000 pushcarts crowded the streets of the Lower East Side in New York City, with vendors selling everything from pots and pans to fruits and vegetables. It was here, gathered around the pushcart, that immigrant Jews came together to debate religion and politics. When Jewish-run delicatessens opened, these same conversations were had around tables there, as people sought out each other's company for a feeling of community, and to be with people like themselves, torn from their homelands.

Page 6: Photo, 1903. Louis and Rebecca Shapiro in their horse-drawn cart selling teas and coffees before opening their well-known delicatessen in Indianapolis, Indiana, two years later. *(Courtesy of Shapiro's Delicatessen)*

Photo, circa 1920. Poultry market on the Lower East Side of New York City. *(Courtesy of Rabbi Peter Schweitzer)*

Cookbook cover, 1933. Proctor & Gamble published a cookbook with recipes to assist Jewish housewives. *(Courtesy of Proctor & Gamble)*

Most deli food is peasant food from the *shtetls* (small villages of Eastern Europe). In the delicatessens, foods of Eastern European Jewry melded with the foods from Lithuania, Russia, and Hungary. Though a large part of the population remained faithful to kosher laws — dietary rules based on the cleanliness of certain foods and their preparations — another segment of the population decided that being kosher would not be helpful in their assimilation into a new country.

The essence of a deli is much more than a steaming bowl of matzo ball soup or crisp savory potato latkes; it is comfort, memories, and nostalgia. We all have a nostalgic food memory that binds us to our childhood. The aroma of matzo ball soup or brisket and potato pancakes can instantly transport me back to 1950, watching my grandmother prepare savory meals and mouthwatering desserts, the likes of which I've never been able to successfully re-create. A favorite memory is of standing at the counter in my grandmother's kitchen, watching her make Romanian eggplant salad. She would roast an eggplant, peel away the skin, and, standing over an old earthenware platter with a large wooden fork in her hand, chop the eggplant for what seemed like hours, adding salt and a little olive oil until the mass of smooth paste clung to the platter. The fork

marks were exact and the salad, sublime. I would wait with great anticipation for her to spread some of the salad onto a slice of rye bread. I don't think I've eaten anything as flavorful since.

Unfortunately, I did not have the foresight to ask my grandmother for her recipes. But, in truth, there most likely were no recipes anyway! Much of the cooking done by immigrants to this country was from memory, tradition, and an innate sense of what their native foods should taste like. My grandmother's recipe for egg custard? "Just put in a little milk and sugar, a little at a time, and a couple of eggs. You'll know when it's right by the way it looks." Sometimes, in speaking with countermen and deli owners throughout the United States while researching this book, I was met with a reluctance to share prized recipes. I believe the reason for this is not that the recipes are secret; it's that the recipes have never been written down. Over and over when inquiring about a recipe, I received the answer that no knish is alike — some are round, some are square; kugels differ from deli to deli; and every bowl of matzo ball soup is unique.

Throughout history, the foods the Jews held so dear were often based on ritual and religion as well as on convenience and necessity. Matzo came about

because the Jews, while fleeing Egypt, had no time to wait for their bread to rise. The idea of the potato latke eaten on Hanukkah came about because the oil that was to burn in the Temple for only one night miraculously lasted for eight days. Oil is celebrated, and one way Jews like to celebrate is with food, and so — the oil-fried latke!

It is important to understand that there have been rules and regulations for the preparation of Jewish food for almost 3,000 years. Kosher law is believed to promote a healthier lifestyle by prohibiting the eating of animals believed to be unclean or killed in an unnatural manner. Early Jewish history describes a tribe with Semitic origins living in the Chaldean region of Egypt, and later in an area known as Goshen, in the northeastern part of Egypt around 1350 B.C.E. It was here the Jews were taken into slavery. Nearly a century later, Moses led these Jews from bondage through the desert to the Holy Land. A significant period began then for the Jews, under the rule of King David. The king's son, Solomon, built the First Temple in Jerusalem. But instead of bringing the people together, the temple served to divide his people. The country broke into two parts, the north becoming known as Israel and the south as Judea. These countries battled fiercely for two centuries, starting around 935 B.C.E.,

which led to the dispersion of the Israelites and the legend of the ten lost tribes of Israel. It is a matter of conjecture as to where the ten tribes dispersed, but it is believed to have been as far as India and China. Another view holds that they turned toward Africa and England. After the Romans took control of Jerusalem in 70 C.E. the city of Jerusalem was destroyed and the Jews dispersed, this time mostly to Europe and Spain.

Further dispersion, or diaspora, came with the Crusades between the eleventh and fourteenth centuries, which enforced a series of laws forcing the Jews from their adopted countries — England in 1290, France in 1392, and Spain in 1492. Many Jews fled to Turkey and Holland, two countries where they were welcomed. Many more settled in Russia, Poland, Austria, Germany, and Romania.

According to Jewish history, Moses gave the earliest laws concerning food to the people prior to leaving Egypt. The five books of the Bible may have also set forth rules regarding kosher law. For our purposes, I merely want to give a brief, if not debatable, reason for how and why Jewish foods have evolved. With few exceptions, such as foods permitted on Passover, kosher Jews abide by these rules. Secular Jews adapt the rules to suit their own desires and lifestyle.

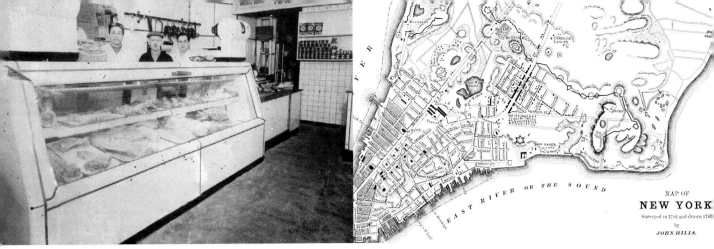

Photo, circa 1940. The kosher meat counter in the market of H. Weinberg and Sons. The business went on to become Empire National in 1951. Pictured, left to right, are Justin Aufseeser, Hugo Weinberg, and Gustav Goetz. *(Courtesy of Empire Kosher)*

Jewish food is broken down into four separate and distinct categories: *Milchig*, or dairy foods (milk, cream, sweet butter, sour cream, buttermilk, cheese), and *Fleishig*, or meat (all meats and organ meats, and poultry, except those classified as *trefe* or prohibited). All Fleishig animals must be killed in accordance with ritual law, and only by a qualified and trained professional, causing the animal as little pain as possible and permitting the maximum effusion of blood. Only the hindquarters can be consumed as they contain fewer veins than the back quarters. The Torah prohibits the consumption of blood as the life of the animal is believed to be contained in the blood. *Parve*, or neutral foods, can be eaten with either meat or dairy. Examples are vegetables and fruits, fish and eggs. *Trefe*, or prohibited foods, include pork and any animal with a cloven hoof. Shellfish is also prohibited. (Only fish with fins and scales are permitted.) These foods are forbidden because they are considered unclean.

It is important to make the distinction between a kosher and a non-kosher delicatessen. Strictly kosher delis abide by the rules of *kashrut* — they are either entirely a meat or a dairy establishment and they often have signage indicating their stamp of kosher approval. Non-kosher delis serve Jewish food but will serve dairy with meat and may serve non-kosher items.

Jewish delis are known for their table or counter service, with countermen dressed in white coats or aprons, which give the impression of sterility. Pickles and coleslaw are regularly set on the table, and unusually edgy waiters serve the standard soups and sandwiches on rye or pumpernickel. A delicatessen features meals like brisket of beef, potato pancakes, cheese blintzes, and matzo ball soup, and for dessert, rich specialties such as cheesecake and rice pudding. You won't find white or sourdough bread here, and mayonnaise will not be served on your corned beef sandwich!

New York and Los Angeles are not the only places delis have thrived throughout the twentieth century. There are several in midwestern and southern states that are worth noting. The Olde Tyme Deli, which was located in Jackson, Mississippi, had a rich past that is explored in this book: before it closed in the 1980s, it served civil rights workers alongside members of the Ku Klux Klan.

The South has had a vibrant Jewish community for generations. Southern Jews assimilated quickly because they were such a distinct minority in

these relatively remote cities and towns. This assimilation was important to bind the Jewish people to their communities. Bagels were served with grits. Matzo balls had a distinct Cajun influence. It was only at events such as weddings and bar and bat mitzvahs, or group gatherings that centered on food, that southern Jews could share in their culture. They would some-times have their corned beef and pastrami sent in from delis as far away as New York City or Boston.

When you enter a deli, the sights, smells, and sounds thrill your senses — from the simple, comforting décor of Formica tables to the pungent odors of pastrami and sour pickles. Here you are family in the best sense of the word. Where else would you know the name of your favorite waitress, have her ask about your children or the health of your parents? This isn't just a job for them; it's their life. Some have worked in the same deli for thirty or forty years.

At one time in New York City, there were 140 Jewish grocers, 131 kosher butcher shops, 100 seltzer bottling plants, 62 candy stores, 36 bakeries, 30 dairy stores, and numerous fish shops, fruit stands, and wine shops. There were six Yiddish newspapers,

500 religious schools and synagogues, and more than twenty theaters. By the mid 1930s, that way of life began to change as Jewish immigrants moved on to other parts of the country. The area lost much of its cultural texture and so many of its touchstones.

Today, deli culture has nearly vanished in much of the South and the Midwest. Even in cities where great delis have long thrived, one by one, delis are starting to close their doors. Darbys and Boesky's in Detroit, Wolfie's in Miami Beach, Ratner's Dairy Restaurant and Gitlitz's in New York City, and The Olde Tyme Deli in Jackson, Mississippi, are all now shuttered. Great delis still exist in Los Angeles and New York, but in other cities across the country the deli has taken on the style of the diner and lost much of its characteristic flair.

Recent years have seen renewed interest in historic multicultural communities, however. The Lower East Side of New York has been designated a state and national historic district and has become a hipster hangout, but a few of the last vestiges of Jewish life still stand today: Katz's Deli; Russ & Daughters Appetizing Store; Streit's Matzo; and Economy Candy, a supplier of delicious sweets for over half a century.

Not only are the delis adapting to cultural changes — providing nontraditional menu items that appeal to health-conscious eaters — but the foods that you once could only find in a Jewish deli are found more and more often on menus at restaurants of all kinds. Today you might find matzo ball soup at a local diner, or brisket at the most elegant restaurant. But in all honesty, it won't taste the same. The deli experience is just like home; it's just that the food's better!

 And that is the reason for this book: to preserve what memories are left of the colorful history of the American Jewish deli, and to make sure that those recipes that, for decades, were passed down by practice and instinct are recorded for the rest of us so that we may enjoy them for decades to come.

This is a history book with recipes from some of the most renowned delis in the United States, showcasing the richness of Jewish food throughout the centuries. Kosher and non-kosher delis alike are included; when possible, I indicate the distinction. Enjoy the food as you enjoy the history — and note that I make no apologies for the fat content; that's just not the point.

My hope is that you will be inspired to start a tradition of your own with the recipes collected here. And the next time you bite into a hot pastrami sandwich slathered with mustard on rye, I hope every sense is heightened as you appreciate the legacy that has been so lovingly preserved and passed on.

THE HISTORY OF DELIS
A TIMELINE
Part I

6000 BCE   4000 BCE   3000 BCE   2030 BCE

Humans as hunters and gatherers gain the knowledge to boil water. And so, borscht is born.

Yeast is used in the making of beer by the Babylonians and Sumerians.

Pickling is used in India as a method of preserving food.

The Egyptians use yeast to bake leavened bread.

Molds are used in cheese making.

Wine and vinegar are fermented using yeast.

Kosher laws are derived from specific instructions in the Torah.

Halvah, the candy made from ground sesame seeds, is created in the Middle East.

The pulp of the horseradish root is consumed in ancient times as an aphrodisiac.

Cucumbers are preserved in the Tigris Valley. Soon, cucumber vines are found throughout Europe.

The first fish drying and smoking station is in operation near the River Bann in Ireland. (This may be the origin of lox.)

Page 14: Postcard, circa 1990. David Tarawsky, an employee at Katz's Deli for 50 years, was still slicing pastrami at the age of 90. *(Courtesy of Katz's Deli)*

Postcard, circa 1890. New York street scene featuring cart peddlers. *(Courtesy of Rabbi Peter Schweitzer)*

1220 BCE

Moses led the Jewish people from bondage in Egypt to begin again in the Holy Land. (Their hasty retreat did not allow time to bake their bread. The dough they carried baked in the hot sun and created what we know today as matzo.)

1290 CE

Jews are forced to leave England by Edward I, making England the first country to expel the Jews. This is the beginning of 350 years of Jewish exile.

1484

The hot dog, or frankfurter, originates in Frankfurt-Am-Main, Germany.

1492

Jews are forced to leave Spain by Queen Isabella, taking with them their knowledge of baking challah, a ritual bread.

Mandelbrot, an almond bread eaten like a cookie, is thought to have been brought to Italy by Spanish Jews.

1520–1600

Rules and regulations regarding food and proper kosher preparation are outlined, expanded, and modified by rabbis as Jews encountered new cultures and circumstances.

Postcard, circa 1870. Immigrants lining up for their entry into America. *(Courtesy of Rabbi Peter Schweitzer)*

1610 — *1654* — *1790* — *1792* —

Bagels are created in Krakow, Poland, and given as gifts to women after childbirth.

Twenty-three Sephardic Jews arrive in New Amsterdam (New York).

Bavarian and Alsatian Jews use sugar to make sweet kugel.

Postcard, circa 1890. The area that is now known as New York Harbor was the first glimpse of America for many immigrants. The Statue of Liberty wasn't there to welcome them until 1886. *(Courtesy of Rabbi Peter Schweitzer)*

Seltzer, or tea water as it was called, is sold from horse-drawn carts in New York City.

Macaroons, which originated in an Italian monastery, are sold throughout Italy. Italian Jews adapt this cookie to meet their dietary needs and pass it on to their Jewish counterparts.

German Jews immigrate to America in great numbers.

Charles Feltman, a German butcher, opens the first Coney Island hot dog stand in Brooklyn, New York.

In Cincinnati, Ohio, business partners Charles and Max Fleischmann and James Goff produce and patent a yeast cake that revolutionizes home baking.

Cel-Ray tonic, a celery-based flavored seltzer drink, is introduced. (This drink gains huge popularity and becomes a quintessential deli drink.)

Soda can, modern. Dr. Brown's Cel-Ray Celery Soda. (Courtesy of Dr. Brown's/Canada Dry Bottling Company)

Postcard, circa 1890. Immigrant ships arriving in America. (Courtesy of Rabbi Peter Schweitzer)

Postcard, circa 1890. A newly arrived immigrant family looking upon the New York City skyline. (Courtesy of Rabbi Peter Schweitzer)

1870

Rokeach Foods is founded in Brooklyn, New York, as a kosher soap company. (It later branches out to produce a variety of kosher food and non-food products.)

Product label, circa 1900. In business since 1870, Rokeach Foods Corporation has supplied delis with its kosher food products for generations and is one of the most trusted names in kosher food companies. Its founder, Israel Rokeach, began marketing gefilte fish, borscht, and jams in glass containers in the early 1900s. He was also the forerunner of the five-day work week.

1872

Cream cheese is perfected, thus making cheesecake possible as well as a new accompaniment for the bagel and lox.

1880s

Jews from Eastern Europe began to immigrate to America in large numbers, fleeing persecution, difficult living conditions, and illness.

Anton Feuchwager, a German peddler, invents the hot dog bun with the help of his brother-in-law, a baker. He originally provided gloves to customers to help them hold the scalding hot dogs but grew tired of the theft of the gloves.

Phenix Cheese Company introduces Philadelphia Brand Cream Cheese.

1881

Yiddish-speaking Jews begin immigrating to New York City and settle on the Lower East Side. Their population reaches 1 million by 1903.

Postcard, circa 1890. A bustling street scene on the Lower East Side of New York City. *(Courtesy of Rabbi Peter Schweitzer)*

1888   1890   1901   1904

Rabbi Dov Behr Manischewitz opens a small matzo bakery in Cincinnati, Ohio. (The Manischewitz Company becomes one of the largest kosher food product distributors in America.)

Katz's Deli opens on Ludlow Street on the Lower East Side and moves across the street to 205 East Houston Street when New York City begins construction of the subway.

The egg cream is invented by Louis Auster at Auster's Candy Shop in New York. (The drink remains a classic deli favorite.)

Flyer art, 1985.

The Settlement Cookbook is published. It was created by Mrs. Simon Kander in Milwaukee, Wisconsin, to benefit The Settlement House, an organization that aided newly arrived immigrants by teaching them the skills necessary to assimilate into the American lifestyle at the turn of the century. (It subsequently became one of the most successful cookbooks of all time.)

Herman Fox develops a recipe for chocolate syrup containing sugar, corn sweetener, cocoa, and his "secret thing" (quite possibly Brooklyn water).

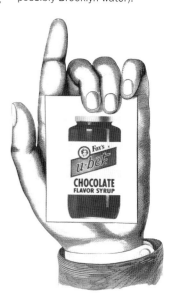

Flyer art, 1985. Part of an advertising flyer offered by Fox's u-bet Syrup to promote its signature brand and key egg cream ingredient, Fox's u-bet Chocolate Syrup. *(Courtesy of Fox's u-bet Syrup)*

Photo, 2000. Coney Island Bialy Bakery benchman Joseph Jackson pours ready-made, hand-rolled bagels into water to boil. The process helps to put moisture in the dough before baking. *(Courtesy of Steve Ross)*

Photo, 1940. Max Shapiro carried on his father's work at Shapiro's Delicatessen. *(Courtesy of Shapiro's Delicatessen)*

Photo, 1990. *(Courtesy of Yonah Shimmel's Knishes)*

1905   1907   1908   1910

Hebrew National Foods produces the first kosher frankfurter.

Ratner's Dairy Restaurant opens on 87 Pitt Street in New York City, serving dairy meals for 25 cents.

Shapiro's Delicatessen opens in Indianapolis, Indiana.

The Bagel Bakers Union #338 is formed, admitting only 300 bakers.

Barney Greengrass (aka The Sturgeon King) opens an appetizing shop in Harlem, New York, and specializes in smoked fish.

Yonah Schimmel, the original snack master, opens Yonah Schimmel Knishes on 137 Houston Street in New York City.

Opposite page: Photo, 1938. Allen Street, teeming with newly arrived immigrants, in New York City's Lower East Side. *(Courtesy of Russ & Daughters Appetizing Store)*

First column: (Top) Logo, 1965 *(Courtesy of Hebrew National, Division of ConAgra Foods)*; (Bottom) Logo, circa 1960. *(Courtesy of the Harmatz family)*

Logo, 2003. A modern variation on the original 1908 Barney Greengrass logo. *(Courtesy of Barney Greengrass)*

Photo, 2001. The historic Russ & Daughters Appetizers building, nearly unchanged since 1914, on the Lower East Side of New York City. *(Courtesy of Joshua Tupper)*

Photo, 1975. Seymour Attman, second-generation owner of Attman's delicatessen. *(Courtesy of Attman's)*

Photo, date unknown. A storefront selling Crisco for 17 cents a container or three containers for 47 cents. *(Courtesy of Proctor & Gamble)*

1910–1911 *1912* *1914* *1915*

Crisco, an all-vegetable shortening, is a boon for the Jewish homemaker. Jewish cooks can use this product for cooking kosher meat and dairy dishes.

The Settlement Cookbook is in its sixth printing.

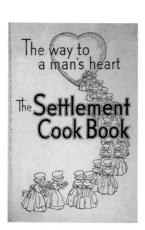

Russ and Daughters Appetizing Store opens at 179 East Houston Street in New York City, selling appetizers such as lox, smoked fish, and herring.

The first Reuben sandwich is named in New York City by Arnold Reuben of Reuben's Deli.

Attman's delicatessen opens on East Baltimore Street in Baltimore, Maryland.

Decorative plate, date unknown. Crisco advertised its product as an alternative to animal fat. *(Courtesy of Proctor & Gamble)*

Cookbook cover, 1949. *(Courtesy of the author)*

1916   1917   1918   1920s

1916

Streit's Matzo Bakery opens on Pitt Street in New York City.

1917

Boesky's Delicatessen opens in Detroit, Michigan.

Lou G. Siegel's Kosher Restaurant and Deli opens in the Garment District in New York City. This deli caters to the workers in the garment trade.

1918

Jacob Harmatz moves Ratner's Dairy Restaurant to 138 Delancy Street in New York City's Lower East Side.

1919

Schnider's Delicatessen opens a small store in Springfield, Massachusetts.

1920s

Herman Fox officially renames his 1904 Fox's Chocolate Syrup Company to Fox's u-bet Syrup. (The syrup becomes the definitive product used in egg cream.)

Photo, 1931. Interior of the first Canter's Deli, where corned beef sandwiches sold for only 10 cents in the early 1930s. *(Courtesy of Canter's Deli)*

Menu art, modern. *(Courtesy of Jeffrey Segal)*

1920

Morris Rosenzweig opens the Coney Island Bialy Bakery in Brooklyn, New York. (It's now a third-generation-owned bagel and bialy bakery.)

1921

Lindy's Delicatessen opens on Broadway in New York City. The deli was later showcased in Damon Runyon's Broadway musical *Guys and Dolls*, referred to there as "Mindy's."

1923

The Famous Fourth Street Deli opens in South Philadelphia, Pennsylvania.

1924

Canter's Deli opens in Jersey City, New Jersey.

Business Card. *(Courtesy of Famous Fourth Street Deli)*

Photo, circa 1940. Exterior of the original Canter's Deli, located in the Boyle Heights section of Los Angeles. *(Courtesy of Canter's Deli)*

Photo, circa 1945. Gold's Horseradish delivery truck. *(Courtesy of Gold's Horseradish)*

1927

Lender's Bagels is founded in New Haven, Connecticut.

Attman's Delicatessen moves to Lombard Street on "corned beef row" in Baltimore, Maryland.

Izzy Guss ventures into the pickle business on the Lower East Side. (Guss' Pickles still sells its signature barrel pickles, now under the name of Ess-a-Pickle.)

1929

Harry Rosen opens the Enduro Restaurant & Nightclub on the corner of Flatbush and DeKalb avenues in Brooklyn, New York.

Barney Greengrass moves his shop to 541 Amsterdam Avenue in New York City.

Eisenberg's Sandwich Shop and Deli opens at 174 Fifth Avenue in New York City.

1931

The Canter brothers open Canter's Deli on Brooklyn Avenue in East Los Angeles, California.

1932

Manischewitz closes its Cincinnati, Ohio, plant and moves to Jersey City, New Jersey.

Gold's Horseradish begins in the kitchen of Tillie Gold's apartment in Coney Island, New York. (It becomes one of the most well-known companies in America.)

Menu, 1989. *(Courtesy of Eisenberg's Sandwich Shop)*

Menu, 1957. *(Courtesy of Barney Greengrass)*

Logo, circa 1950. Gold's Horseradish jars are still a familiar sight behind deli counters. *(Courtesy of Gold's Horseradish)*

Postcard, circa 1890. Newly arrived immigrants waiting to be processed at Ellis Island. *(Courtesy of Rabbi Peter Schweitzer)*

Photo, circa 1945. Max Asnas and a counterman in front of Stage Deli's new Seventh Avenue location. *(Courtesy of Stage Deli)*

1937

The Coca-Cola Company is the first beverage company to obtain kosher certification. This certification brings the world's most popular drink to Jewish homes.

The Carnegie Deli opens at 854 Seventh Avenue in New York City.

Max Asnas's original Stage Delicatessen opens on Broadway and 48th Street in New York City.

Economy Candy opens on Rivington Street on the Lower East Side of New York City, supplying many delis and walk-in customers with tasty halvah.

1938

Empire Kosher Poultry, Inc. is started in the Catskills in upstate New York. (It evolves to become the world's largest kosher poultry processing plant.)

1940

Manischewitz introduces its Tam Tam Crackers, its first departure from standard matzo.

The Settlement Cookbook sells its 500,000th copy.

1943

Stage Delicatessen moves to Seventh Avenue in New York City.

Second column (top): Photo, circa 1975. Carnegie Deli exterior, unchanged since its opening in 1937. The location near Carnegie Hall makes it a hangout for musicians, locals, and tourists alike. Second column (bottom): Logo, 2000. Economy Candy is still owned by its founding family, the Cohens, and it remains a mainstay candy store for many New Yorkers.

Cookbook cover, 1965. *(Courtesy of the author)*

Photo, circa 1950. Stage Deli owner, Max Asnas, surrounded by his trusty countermen. *(Courtesy of Stage Deli)*

Photo, 1947. Exterior of Nate 'n Al's Delicatessen on Beverly Boulevard in Beverly Hills, California. *(Courtesy of Nate 'n Al's Delicatessen)*

Product label, 2003. *(Courtesy of Empire National)*

1945

Nate 'n Al's opens at 414 North Beverly Drive in Los Angeles, California.

Mac's Delicatessen opens in El Paso, Texas.

1947

Langer's Delicatessen opens on the corner of Seventh Avenue and Alvarado in Los Angeles, California.

1950

The Enduro Restaurant & Nightclub reopens as Junior's Delicatessen.

1951

Empire National begins to make kosher beef products in the Bronx, New York.

1946

Thousands of Holocaust survivors begin to arrive in America.

1948

Factor's Famous Deli opens at 9420 West Pico Boulevard in Los Angeles, California.

Menu art, 1960s. *(Courtesy of Rita Silverman)*   Logo, 2003. *(Courtesy of Factor's Famous Deli)*   Menu, 2002. *(Courtesy of Junior's)*

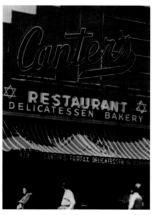

Photo, circa 1950s. Canter's Deli's new Fairfax location. *(Courtesy of Canter's Deli)*

Photo, circa 1960. *(Courtesy of 2nd Avenue Deli)*

Photo, 2004. The famed Rose's neon sign welcomes diners to the deli. *(Courtesy of Rose's Deli)*

Photo, circa 1970. Morris Gottesman and Abe Lebewohl behind the 2nd Avenue Deli counter and ready to serve the public. *(Courtesy of 2nd Avenue Deli)*

1953 · · · · · 1954 · · · · · 1956 · · · · · 1957 · · · · ·

1953

Canter's Deli moves to 419 Fairfax in Los Angeles, California.

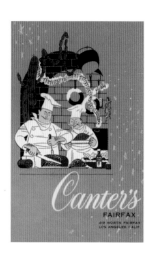

Menu, 1955. *(Courtesy of Canter's Deli)*

1954

ACME

Acme Smoked Fish Corporation opens in Brooklyn, New York.

Protzel's Delicatessen opens near St. Louis, Missouri.

The 2nd Avenue Deli opens at 156 Second Avenue on the corner of Tenth Street in New York City.

Manischewitz begins to manufacture canned and jarred products.

Logo, 1994. Acme Smoked Fish Corporation has been in business since 1913, providing fresh fish and other seafood to delis on the East Coast. *(Courtesy of ACME Smoked Fish Corporation)*

1956

DARBYS

Darbys delicatessen opens in Detroit, Michigan.

Rose Naftalin opens a small deli in Portland, Oregon.

Corky & Lenny's opens in a suburb of Cleveland, Ohio.

Menu art, 1956. Part of the Darbys logo as seen on an original 1956 menu. *(Courtesy of Rhonda Kerner)*

1957

Art's Deli opens to serve the movie and television trade in Studio City, California.

Menu art, 1994. The menu at Art's Deli has never changed — only the prices have! *(Courtesy of Art's Deli)*

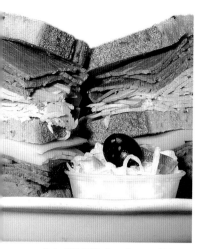

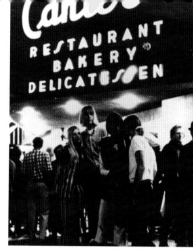

Photo, 2005. Not for the weak — a sandwich combination of corned beef, pastrami, and turkey. *(Courtesy of Jay Heyman)*

Photo, 2000. Neon sign at Coney Island Bialy Bakery, where bialys have been hand-rolled since 1920. They began producing bagels by hand in 1960. *(Courtesy of Steve Ross)*

Menu, 1956. *(Courtesy of Rhonda Kerner)*

Photo, circa 1960s. When the Kibbitz Room opened in Canter's Deli, many of the psychedelic crowd came to listen to music. *(Courtesy of Canter's Deli)*

1961

The Olde Tyme Deli, the only Jewish deli in Mississippi, opens in Jackson.

1965

Hebrew National hot dogs launch the ad campaign "We answer to a higher authority" to appeal to Jews and non-Jews alike. It quickly becomes a symbol of quality for all consumers.

1972

Ben's Kosher Delicatessen opens at 209 West 38th Street in New York City.

1980

D. Z. Akin's Deli opens its doors in San Diego, California, to a very hungry populace.

1962

Lender's Bagels buys the first bagel machine, which leads to expansion and production of the first mass-produced frozen bagels.

1968

The landmark Darbys in Detroit, Michigan, burns to the ground. It never reopens; a legend is lost.

1973

Junior's cheesecake is rated #1 cheesecake by *New York Magazine*.

1981

Fire consumes Junior's Restaurant.

Logo, 1961. This logo appeared on The Olde Tyme Deli menu during its heyday. *(Courtesy of Irving Feldman)*

Logo, 2003. *(Courtesy of Ben's Kosher Delicatessen)*

Menu art, 1985.

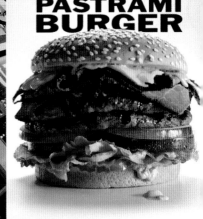

1982   1987   1995   2004

Junior's reopens on May 27th.

Zingerman's Delicatessen opens in Ann Arbor, Michigan.

Kosher Cajun New York Deli & Grocery opens outside of New Orleans, Louisiana.

Bagel sales outnumber donut sales in California.

Canter's Deli opens a branch of the deli in Las Vegas, Nevada, at the Treasure Island Resort Hotel.

1993   2002   2005   2006/2007

Gold's Pure Foods begins producing coarse deli mustard served in delis.

Canter's Deli opens a branch of the deli in Las Vegas, Nevada, at the Treasure Island Resort Hotel and more recently at the Mandalay Bay Hotel in Las Vegas and Dodgers Stadium in Los Angeles.

Carl's Jr. unveils The Pastrami Burger™, an all-beef patty topped with thinly sliced pastrami.

Sadly, the 2nd Avenue Deli closed its doors in January 2006 after 52 years on Second Avenue in New York City. Happily, it re-opened in December 2007 (on East 33rd Street), and may it be there another fifty years.

DELI FOOD HISTORIES
FROM CHOPPED LIVER TO CHEESECAKE
Part II

Photo, 2000. A sheet of fresh, hot bialys at Coney Island Bialy Bakery. *(Courtesy of Steve Ross)*

Bagel

Bagel purists, revolt! What was once the icon of urban New York City delis is no longer. The original bagel — the hard, crusty, plain roll — has become softer, bigger, and lighter, and is sometimes fruit-flavored, covered in seeds, and even red or green!

The original bagel is made from flour, salt, water, yeast, and malt. To gelatinize the starch, the bagel is first boiled in order to make the dough stretchy, so that it can rise and form a shiny crust while baking. Special measures were implemented in 1907 when the bagel baker's local #338 was formed, allowing only 300 bakers to keep the recipe tradition alive and safeguarded.

Bagels have a long and colorful history. Research indicates that in 1610, in Krakow, Poland, *beygls*, as they were called, were given as gifts to women after childbirth. Then, according to legend, around 1683 a Viennese baker paid tribute to King Sobieski of Poland with a beygl variation. The king had saved the Austrian people from Turkish invaders, and since he was a great horseman, the baker shaped the dough into an uneven circle resembling a stirrup, or *beugal*.

The modern bagel arrived in America in the early 1880s with a wave of Eastern European Jewish immigrants. Not long after that, cream cheese was developed and lox met its mate. Today, bagels are more popular than donuts and are enjoyed around the world. Eaten with any number of spreads and treatments, from the traditional cream cheese or butter to toasting and sandwich fixings, bagels are now one of the most popular of all convenience foods.

Page 34: Photo, 1953. The fully stocked deli counter at Canter's Deli on Fairfax Avenue in Los Angeles, California — the pastrami, hot dogs, pickles, cheeses, herring, and fishes all lined up and looking beautiful. *(Courtesy of Canter's Deli)*

Bialy

A poor cousin of the bagel, the bialy is a round, flat-bottomed, onion-topped roll without the distinctive hole of the bagel. The bialy is best eaten fresh and is tastiest served warm. Like a bagel, it is delicious spread with cream cheese or butter but is traditionally not sliced like the bagel, as the bialy is too thin.

The origin of the word *bialy* is debatable. Some think it comes from Bialystok, Poland. Others believe the bialy comes from Russia, but Poland was Russian at various times in its history, so you can make your own judgments. What we know is that the bialy was formerly called *Bialystok kuchen*.

The bialy is made by hand, rolled, then flattened and pressed in the middle by the baker's thumb to form a gentle indentation that will hold sliced onions, minced garlic, and poppy seeds.

Black and White Cookie

A large, round, cake-like yellow cookie, iced half with white icing and half with chocolate icing, the black and white cookie is believed to be a metaphor for racial harmony. This cookie was thought to have originated in the beginning of the twentieth century by a baker who needed to use up his yellow cake batter. No one knows the true origin, but anyone who has enjoyed one — they are sold at the bakery counters of bakeries and delicatessens — knows that black and white cookies are a treat not to be missed.

Blintzes

Jewish tradition pairs specific foods with
particular holidays. On Hanukkah, it's potato
latkes. Purim is celebrated with the triangular
filled cookie, Hamentashen. On Passover, leavened
products and legumes are prohibited by Jewish law.
On Shavuot, it's customary to serve dairy dishes,
and cheese blintzes are the food of choice.

There's a bit of history and a lot of mythology
surrounding the blintz, a thin pancake wrapped
around a filling. Like the French crêpe, many fillings work with blintzes. Some blintzes are *pareve*,
meaning they can be made with either potatoes
or with a fruit filling. Blintzes are suitable for
breakfast, or as an accompanying side dish, main
course, or dessert. Most blintzes found in delis
are sweet rather than savory, filled with fruit or
farmer's cheese, and topped with a fruit filling
or a sprinkle of powdered sugar.

The blintz is most likely a Polish invention,
brought to this country by Polish immigrants. The
word *blini* is Slavic, and describes the buckwheat
pancake that Russians serve with melted butter
and, sometimes, caviar. An old folk tale tells of a
young Russian Jew recruited into Stalin's secret
police. When someone attempted to poison Stalin's
food, Stalin had all six of his chefs executed, and
he appointed this young boy as his replacement
chef. The boy knew only two recipes, for latkes
and for blintzes, and he claims that Stalin became
so fond of his cooking that he was hired as his
personal chef.

Borscht

Historically called the Russian bowl of plenty, this
soup — with origins in
Russia or Poland — is
typically made from
fresh beets. It can
also be made using a
combination of vegetables
or meat and meat stock.
Borscht is served hot or
cold and is garnished
with a dollop of sour
cream or a chopped hard-
boiled egg.

Challah

No single food carries the significance of tradition like challah, a slightly sweet, shiny, braided egg bread. *Challah* comes from the Hebrew word for portion and symbolizes all that is sacred to the Jewish people. The German-Jewish name for this traditional ritual bread used to be *berches* and is believed to have originated in southern Germany in the Middle Ages.

In the fifteenth century, as Jewish people moved east from Spain, Italy, and Portugal, they took this ritual bread with them. It is said that the shape of the braided challah resembles the hair of a Polish maiden for whom the baker of the challah had an unrequited passion. To him the braid was the most beautiful shape he could imagine for his bread.

When baking challah, Jewish law dictates that you remove a token amount of dough, about the size of an olive, and burn it while reciting a prayer. Now a symbolic gesture, this was once an offering to the priests of the First Temple. The challah is then covered to represent the dew that collected on the manna the morning that the Jewish people made their exodus from Egypt.

Challah is a staple in delis, and you'll find it sold there in various symbolic shapes for use as a sandwich bread, a base to French toast, or simply sliced to accompany a hot bowl of soup. Braided challah have three, four, or six intertwined strands meant to symbolize love. Three braids symbolize truth, peace, and justice. Round loaves baked on the Jewish High Holy Days are meant to show that there is no beginning and no end, that the coming year should be free of tragedy, and to symbolize continuity. Challah that look like ladders signify the hope to ascend to great heights, while challah baked in the shape of a hand denotes hope of being inscribed for a good year; this challah is served before the traditional fast on Yom Kippur. Other shapes are triangular for Purim, symbolizing Hamman's hats, and two shaped like tablets, signifying the Ten Commandments. Lithuanian Jews topped their challah with a crown as a testament to God, and in the Ukraine, the challah was baked in the shape of a bird to offer protection.

Cheesecake

Cheesecake is as rich in history as it is in flavor, and it is a classic finish to any deli meal.

The origins of cheesecake date back to ancient Greece, when it was baked in the shape of a woman's breast and served to Olympic athletes during the games in 776 B.C.E. That explains how the word "cheesecake" came to refer to pin-up girls in decades past. Early Jewish immigrants used a combination of pot cheese and cream cheese, which resulted in a heavier, denser cheesecake.

New York cheesecake is a dense and creamy balance of tart and sweet contained in five simple ingredients: cream cheese, sugar, eggs, vanilla, and heavy cream. It's been made famous in restaurants like Lindy's, Junior's, and Stage Deli.

Chopped Liver

We've all heard the expression "What am I, chopped liver?" when someone wants to indicate a feeling of being viewed as less than great. How can this be? Chopped liver tastes too good to be thought of this way!

Chopped liver is a made from a combination of ground chicken (and sometimes calf) liver, sautéed onions, hard-boiled eggs, and schmaltz (chicken fat, or "Jewish butter"). It is high in protein and iron and is loaded with cholesterol. This rich and indulgent food is often served as an appetizer on matzo or sliced rye bread or eaten piled high on a sandwich, sometimes accompanied with corned beef. Chopped liver has a lumpy consistency, is hardly an elegant pâté, and is definitely an acquired taste.

Chopped liver has its roots in medieval times in Strasbourg and the Alsace, and was at that time made from goose livers. The use of chicken livers came later and was an Eastern European delicacy. Mounds of this food can be found served on appetizer platters at Jewish weddings and bar and bat mitzvah celebrations. Only eat it on special occasions — along with your tummy and your tastebuds, your heart and arteries will thank you!

Corned Beef

Does size matter? Apparently bigger is better when it comes to the corned beef sandwich served in delis across America. Many delis are judged by the size of their oversized corned beef sandwich. Sayings like "You'll need a knife and fork!" or "Don't attempt it any other way or you'll dislocate your jaw!" appear on menus from New York to Los Angeles.

The term "corned" dates back long before refrigeration. The meat was dry-cured in cement tanks or wooden barrels and then coarse "corn" — large, corn-sized pellets of salt — were rubbed into the meat to preserve it. Butcher shops in the early 1900s relied on salt as a means of preserving. They closed on weekends and needed a way to keep the beef fresh other than using ice, which was quite undependable. The butcher would soak the meat in a strong brine or cover it with coarse salt to promote "osmosis" (the process of water and salt infusing into the meat). Today, brining with the use of salt water has replaced the salt cure method, but the name "corned beef" is still used. Modern corned beef is made from brisket of beef, the more tender, flavorful, and fatty cut of choice. The meat is injected with flavorings and cured, or "corned," in a brine for several days. Peppercorns, bay leaves, garlic, thyme, mustard seed, salt, and coriander give corned beef its unique flavor, and may very well be the secret to the preparation.

One of the realities of deli cuisine, and most especially of deli meats, is that the flavor of the meat is in the fat. An extra-lean cut, often thought of today as less caloric, is simply not as flavorful. So if you're going to indulge in the deli-eating experience, do it right and enjoy a hearty corned beef sandwich every once in a while.

Cream Cheese

Cream cheese is made from cream that has been dried so that it can be cut with a knife. Cream cheese may have its roots as far back as 9000 B.C.E., when nomadic tribes discovered that the milk they transported would first sour and then separate, through evaporation, leaving a dried curd. A type of cream cheese was first enjoyed by the Greeks and Romans and then by the Europeans.

But it was not until the late nineteenth century that cream cheese as we know it today was first manufactured in this country, in upstate New York. In 1872 dairyman William A. Lawrence set out to duplicate the French cheese Neufchatel. Within a decade, his methods of production were acquired by C. D. Reynolds, who purchased the Empire Cheese Company. The name Philadelphia Brand Cream Cheese was arrived at simply because that city was synonymous with high-quality foods. Kraft Cheese Company entered the cream cheese market in 1924, patenting a method to extend the shelf life from two weeks to four months through pasteurization. With this development, cheesecake made with cream cheese was born. This dry, easily spread curd has since become the "schmeer" we enjoy on bagels today.

Product label, circa 1900.

Photo, 1990. At Katz's Deli in New York City you'll find it all — pastrami, corned beef, tomatoes and coleslaw, and, of course, pickles! *(Courtesy of Yura Dashevsky)*

Dill Pickle

The pickle, noted in West Asian, ancient Egyptian, and Greek history, was born out of the necessity to have preserved foods. It could be over 4,000 years old! Cleopatra attributed her beauty to the effects of pickles. She consumed them regularly, believing she would absorb some of the preservative powers. Legend has it she was buried with thousands of jars of pickles and sealed with a curse. The writings of Pliny the Elder, an ancient author and scientist, mention preserved cucumbers, and it was said that the Roman Emperor Tiberius consumed them on a daily basis, as did Julius Caesar and King John. Early thoughts on the cucumber and its medicinal properties are mentioned in the Bible. Christopher Columbus brought them to America, as he was known to have grown cucumbers in Haiti.

America's commercial pickle industry began in 1659 in New York City when pickles were cured in Brooklyn and sold from barrels on pushcarts. Selling for a nickel each, New York's first commercial pickle district on the Lower East Side fueled pickle wars. With the exception of Guss' Pickles (now called Ess-a-Pickle and located in the Borough Park section of Brooklyn), pickle mongers have become a dying breed. Guss' has been preserving and selling pickles from

barrels since the early twentieth century, using the same slow process that has been in existence for centuries.

Commercial pickling is rapid and done by heating the cucumbers versus soaking them. This causes the cucumbers to soften as the brine seeps in and it ages them within two to three days. Low on texture, taste, and nutrition, these pickles are usually sold in jars at supermarkets.

Traditional delis will have nothing to do with pickles in jars. Expect your own bowl of the slow-cured delights at the table when you sit down.

Original drawing, date unknown. A drawing of the famous Guss' Pickles. The title character in the movie *Crossing Delancy* was a pickle monger modeled after Izzy Guss. *(Courtesy of Tim Baker)*

Guss' Pickles

The pickle has a long and storied history, and Guss' Pickles originally on the Lower East Side of New York has the story! Izzy Guss, who emigrated from Poland in the beginning of the twentieth century, began as an apprentice to an already established pickle monger, Louis Hollander, in 1919. Hollander offered Izzy a pushcart and the knowledge of pickling. Izzy had been in the leather trade in Poland, but he learned quickly and soon ventured into running his own pickle business on Hester Street in 1920. There was plenty of room for competition at that time, as the Lower East Side had the largest concentration of pickle stores in the United States.

Pickles were popular for many reasons. Besides being nutritious and filling, the cucumbers used to make them were easy to obtain. Many Eastern European immigrants already knew the art of pickling as that was something done routinely at home to preserve foods.

Hester and Essex Streets were the main locations for pickle dealers. The cucumbers were shipped from New Jersey via the Hudson River to the large indoor wholesale market on Ludlow Street, where they were readily accessible to pickle brokers.

Pickling brine includes coriander, mustard seed, bay leaf, garlic, hot peppers, and sea salt. Guss' exact recipe is a strictly guarded secret, but the same four types of processing are involved. The new dill is pickled for a short seven to fourteen days in the refrigerator; the half sour is pickled for either two weeks in the refrigerator or two days at room temperature, and then refrigerated until sold; the three-quarter dill pickle is pickled for a month and refrigerated; and, finally, the full sour dill pickle — the granddaddy of pickles — requires a three-month minimum to reach maturity. The acid from the brine soaks in, preserving the pickles and preventing the growth of bacteria. No chemicals, preservatives, or heat is used. A saltometer is used in a controlled environment to check the density of the salt solution; this is key to the success of the pickles.

Izzy Guss employed many family members, including his children and grandchildren. After his death in 1974, his brother, Benny, ran the pickle store on Essex Street. (Benny sold his interest in 1979.) Today, the original and authentic Guss' Pickles have changed their venerable name and are now known as Ess-a-Pickle. They have closed their shop on Orchard Street with the legendary pickle barrels on the outside and have moved inside in the Borough Park section of Brooklyn.

Advertisement, 1980. Dr. Brown's cola is THE drink to accompany a pastrami sandwich. (Courtesy of Dr. Brown's/Canada Dry Bottling Company)

Photo, 1929. (Courtesy of Fox's u-bet Syrup)

Dr. Brown's Cel-Ray Soda

Some say nothing goes better with a corned beef sandwich than a Cel-Ray soda. This classic deli drink is seltzer with an edge. It's celery-flavored, and it's green! Although it is an acquired taste, people who love it swear by it.

Until artificial flavors were invented, all sodas were vegetable flavored. Cel-Ray is the last remaining link to a past where vegetable-flavored sodas were popular. This thirst-quenching drink — an infusion of celery seeds, sugar, and seltzer — was developed in 1869 by a physician treating immigrant children in the Williamsburg section of Brooklyn, New York. It may even have a medicinal effect. The drink was originally called Celery Tonic, but some fifty years ago the government objected to the word "tonic," and the name Cel-Ray was adopted.

Today Dr. Brown's soda comes in other flavors like black cherry, cream soda, and root beer.

Egg Cream

In 1890 in a Brooklyn candy shop, Louis Auster, a Jewish immigrant from Eastern Europe, developed a unique drink devoid of eggs and cream but containing special secret ingredients. Some say it was a witty way to describe richness at a time when no one could afford the luxury of using eggs and cream together in a drink. At one point, Auster declined an offer to sell the recipe rights to a well-known ice cream company, and consequently suffered a slanderous accusation concerning his ethnicity. He vowed then to take the recipe to his grave, and he did just that.

Sometime in the 1920s another gentleman claimed the origination as his own. But this was not without problems, as the syrup wars had begun. Since only syrup, seltzer, and milk are the ingredients of the egg cream, there was a fight to control the syrup trade. Soda fountains went on to sell their own versions of the egg cream, and finally, a formula for the perfect egg cream was settled upon. The accepted recipe featured Fox's u-bet Chocolate Syrup.

The syrup of choice was developed in a Brooklyn basement in the early 1900s. Story has it that Herman Fox, the syrup's developer, followed an urge to pursue his dream of drilling for oil in Texas. When he returned to New York, having failed in his attempt, he brought back the phrase "you bet," which he stamped on his syrup bottles.

You can find egg creams today on a few deli menus as well as bottled and in local specialty food markets.

Above: (Top) Logo, circa early 1900s. This fifth-generation, family-owned company, H. Fox & Company, has been making its fat-free u-bet Chocolate Syrup for more than 100 years. (Bottom) Product label, circa 1920s. *(Courtesy of Fox's u-bet Syrup)*

Flyer, 1985. *(Courtesy of Fox's u-bet Syrup)*

Photo, 1960. Exterior photo of the Fox's u-bet Syrup plant in its original location in Brooklyn, New York.

New York Egg Cream

This is the famous New York Egg Cream, preferably made with Fox's u-bet Chocolate Syrup, but any quality chocolate syrup would work. Seltzer from a pasteurized cylinder is best and renders the most foam. When made correctly, this is a beautiful drink.

> 2 tablespoons Fox's u-bet Chocolate Syrup
>
> 1/2 cup very cold whole milk
>
> 1 cup cold seltzer from a pasteurized cylinder

Pour the milk into a tall 16-ounce (2-cup) glass. Pour in chocolate syrup without stirring. Place a spoon in the glass and spray in cold seltzer over the spoon handle and/or into the sides of the glass (to reduce excess foam) until the foam reaches just below the rim of the glass. Stir gently at first, then more vigorously, until the foam head (key to the egg cream) is stabilized and the syrup is thoroughly mixed. The drink should settle into several shades of light and dark chocolate. Stir and serve immediately with a straw.

Serves 1

Farfel

Farfel, also known as egg barley because of their size and shape, are small dumplings made of egg noodle dough. *Farfallen*, a Yiddish word, means fallen away, which is what happens to the dough when it is grated. It is believed that these tiny dumplings represent fertility and their round shape symbolizes a well-rounded year. Farfel is often served as a side dish or used in soups.

Gefilte Fish

Gefilte (pronounced *geh-fil-teh*) fish is a cold dish made from a mixture of ground whitefish, carp, or pike mixed with eggs, matzo meal, and seasonings. The mixture is formed into balls or patties that are simmered in vegetable or fish stock. The name comes from the Yiddish term for stuffed (*gefüllte*) fish. Originally, the forcemeat, a mixture of carp and pike, was stuffed back into the body of the fish for cooking. Gefilte fish is commonly served on holidays, particularly at Passover, and on the Sabbath. The Russian gefilte fish is more peppery and the Polish variation, sweet. Gefilte fish is usually served sliced, with horseradish as a complementary contrast.

Photo, 1951. The lucky winner of the 1951 Miss Joyva Bathing Beauty Contest held in New York City. *(Courtesy of Joyva)*

Easel-back sign, circa 1950. This vintage stand-up sign for Joyva Halvah features the brand's famous, symbolic Turkish logo, advertising the sweet Middle Eastern candy. *(Courtesy of Joyva)*

Photo, 1953. A billboard, advertising the Joyva Halvah Company, hangs above a street in Manhattan. *(Courtesy of Joyva)*

Gefilte fish has a long history. In the late Middle Ages, Jews began utilizing freshwater fish from the many rivers that crossed their landlocked homes. The wealthy ate carp and pike and the poor ate tench and chub. Carp was introduced from China to Eastern and Central Europe in the seventeenth century, and Jews first farmed the fish in Poland, Lithuania, and the Ukraine. Because gefilte fish is made in advance, Jews were able to eat fish on Shabbat. All the work was already done and one did not have to separate the bones from the fish (as that was considered work, and work was forbidden on the Sabbath).

Halvah

Halvah is a ubiquitous candy sold from the deli counter as if it were a piece of fish or a slice of lox. Hailing from the Middle East and made from ground sesame seed and honey, the confection is cut from a large wheel and sold by the pound. No one knows why halvah is sold in gigantic blocks; perhaps it is because it is more economical to produce it in bulk. This candy, which dates back to

3000 B.C.E might well be the most nutritious candy in the world. Halvah literally means "sweetmeat" in Turkish. Like meat, it contains protein, fat, and carbohydrates, and unlike meat, the fat comes from the seeds.

Halvah's taste and texture is unique. Often called Brooklyn caviar because of its unique ingredients, some describe it as sweet and nutty, with a texture that resembles sawdust or mortar. Others say it compares to a smooth Butterfinger bar. No bar or bat mitzvah is complete without a mountain of halvah to complete the sweet tables.

Joyva, the largest producer of halvah in the United States, opened its doors in 1906 in New York City, on the Lower East Side's popular Orchard Street. Owner Nathan Radutzky, an immigrant from Kiev, began with only a recipe for this nutritious candy and the hope to bring it to the public. In 1951, the Joyva Halvah Company made this sweet available in cans for easier, neater, and faster consumption. You can buy it in bars now, but it's not as much fun!

Flyer, 1951. This application was issued to enter Loew's Bathing Beauty Contest to select Miss Joyva of 1951. *(Courtesy of Joyva)*

Product label, circa 1950. *(Courtesy Gold's Horseradish)*

Horseradish

Besides being the bitter herb used to spice up gefilte fish during Passover, this mysterious 3,000-year-old plant has been used as an aphrodisiac and a treatment for rheumatism. The Egyptians knew of this prized plant by 1500 B.C.E., and early Greeks applied it to the lower back to aid in pain relief. By the time *meerrettich*, as it was called by the Germans, or sea radish, because it grows by the sea, arrived in Eastern Europe it was known as horseradish ("horse" because it denotes the large size and coarseness, and "radish" meaning "root" in Latin). This popular accompaniment for fish or meat finally made its way across the ocean to America by 1806.

In 1930, in Coney Island, New York, a young man was grinding and selling horseradish, also known as *chrain*, from a pushcart on the streets when an altercation broke out between him and the owner of the property on which he was standing. The two men were sent to jail, and after the unfortunate experience the young man wanted nothing more to do with the horseradish grinder or the horseradish business. His cousin Hyman Gold mentioned the problem to his wife, Tillie, and with classic female ingenuity, she insisted the horseradish grinder be brought to her home and into her kitchen. It was there that she and her husband began to produce Gold's Horseradish. They cleaned, cut, and ground the horseradish root and added vinegar to preserve the pungent flavor. They measured it into jars, pasted labels onto the bottles, and took them to the local stores a few at a time so that they would always arrive fresh. Their windows were open wide around the clock, winter and summer, as the strong aroma from this root was impossible to tolerate. Gold's still produces some of the tastiest horseradish on the market.

Jewish Rye Bread

Rye bread is most often the bread of choice in a Jewish deli. People have been eating rye in some form for around three thousand years. Rye is a weed that overtook the wheat field in Northern Europe in the seventeenth century, and when farmers eventually yielded to it, rye became the principal grain of Northern Europe.

In Jewish bakeries in the United States, rye flour and wheat flour are mixed together to produce a rye bread that is lighter in color and texture than the rye breads of Eastern Europe. In Eastern Europe, "Jewish rye" is black bread like the pumpernickel of today; it is dark and dense. There is Polish Jewish rye, which is lighter in color and texture than the other type of Eastern European Jewish rye, and Russian rye is even darker and denser. The rye bread found in most delis in America is the Polish Jewish rye with a chewy flavorful crust.

The rye flour of earlier times was much more flavorful, as the germ and the bran were left in and the proportion of rye to wheat flour was much lower. Today, we rely on the caraway seeds used in many rye breads to get the pungency of flavor we've come to know and enjoy. The naturally sour starter, the catalyst to making the bread rise, is another contributor to the variances in taste between ryes today. Milk is never used, making it parve and therefore accessible to those who prefer a kosher lifestyle.

Dark or light, seeded or unseeded, this rye bread, which is baked and then steamed to give it its chewy texture, is the bread by which all Jewish delis are judged.

Photo, 2005. A pastrami on rye at Rose's Deli in Portland, Oregon. *(Courtesy of Rose's Deli)*

Photo, 1966. A knish pushcart on the Lower East Side of New York City. *(Courtesy of the author)*

Kasha Varnishkes

Kasha, also known as buckwheat, was a mainstay of poor nineteenth-century Russian, Ukrainian, and Polish Jews. It is a hearty grain that sustained them during the long, cold winters. The combination of bow-tie pasta, kasha, and mushrooms make this a popular deli dish.

Kishka

Kishka is an Eastern European-derived sausage made from casings filled with a mixture of bread crumbs or flour, chicken or goose fat, and minced onion. This fatty dish is fast disappearing in the United States due to the unavailability of the casings. However, delis still offer this as an entrée or sliced and eaten with bread. Kishka was a popular appetizer served at weddings and bar mitzvahs, as it is easily eaten as a finger food.

Around 3000 B.C.E., in Iraq and Libya, beef, organ meats, and fat were ground up and encased in the animal intestines, and the sausage was created. This may be one of the first prepared foods.

Knish

A knish is a piece of rectangular or round dough filled with meat, cheese, potato, and, in recent years, chocolate and fruit. It is always baked and can be eaten as a snack or a meal. The earliest form of the knish was primarily a dough pocket filled with cooked grains and baked. Potato fillings were introduced in the sixteenth century.

By 1890, knishes were sold from pushcarts on the streets of the Lower East Side of New York. The knish was the quintessential New York City street food, and it was enjoyed for decades until Mayor Rudy Giuliani applied new restrictions in 1999. Carts did not maintain a steady 140 degrees, and the knishes could spoil and be a health hazard. Thankfully, knishes can still be found in delis, a few remaining knisheries, and specialty grocery stores.

Photo, 2000. The ultimate in dining: three hot dogs with all the essential trimmings — cheese, chili, or sauerkraut. *(Courtesy of Nathan's Famous)*

Photo, circa 1960. Finished matzo cooling on racks while being watched carefully by rabbis.

Photo, 1923. The first Nathan's Famous hot dog stand in Coney Island, New York, where it remains today. Two-year-old Murry, son of the founder, Nathan Handwerker, is on the left, being held up for the camera. *(Courtesy of Nathan's Famous)*

Kosher Hot Dog

Although sausages in some form have been around for centuries, the frankfurter appears to date back to 1484. Some 400 years later, a German butcher named Charles Feltman opened a hot dog stand on Coney Island in Brooklyn, New York, and was credited with putting the hot dog on a warm roll. In 1903, at the St. Louis Louisiana Purchase Exposition, Anton Feuchtwanger introduced the hot dog bun. He had been serving the popular "hot sausages" and handing out white gloves to protect the hands of his patrons, but the gloves kept disappearing. Frustrated by the frequent disappearance of his gloves, Feuchtwanger employed his brother-in-law, a baker, to improvise a long, soft roll to hold the meat, and the modern hot dog bun was born.

In 1916, a former apprentice of Feltman's, Nathan Handwerker, and his wife, Ida, began selling nickel hot dogs at what he called a "hot dog stand" on Coney Island. Today, the landmark "Nathan's Famous" still stands. It has been the favorite of kings, queens, presidents, and celebrities since it introduced its famous spicy hot dog to the world. This was not a kosher hot dog, but it was all beef, which contributed to its general appeal.

Kreplach

Is it a wonton? Is it a pierogi? No — it's a kreplach! And do not confuse them.

A kreplach is a heavy Jewish dumpling that is made from dough, stuffed with meat or cheese and boiled or fried. Shaped like a lumpy, triangular pillow, it is served most often in chicken soup as an alternative to the matzo ball. These triangular dumplings symbolize Judaism's three patriarchs: Abraham, Isaac, and Jacob. In twelfth century Western Europe, these dumplings were filled with meat; in the Slavic lands, they were filled with cheese.

Kugel

Noodles were a staple of the Ashkenazi kitchen, and were used in the preparation of  the kugel. Kugel (pronounced *koo-gl*) is a sweet noodle pudding bound by eggs and baked until firm and crispy. The Polish version is typically sweetened with raisins and seasoned with cinnamon, and

Photo, 1950. The popular hot dog stand, in its signature locale on the corner on Surf and Stillwell avenues in the heart of Coney Island, is a 1950s hotspot. *(Courtesy of Nathan's Famous)*

Photo, 2000. *(Courtesy of Nathan's Famous)*

the Hungarian version of a kugel contains sugar and sour cream and is topped with any manner of toppings including cornflakes, sour cream, cottage cheese, jam, and pineapple. A kugel broke up the monotony of eating potatoes every day.

The first kugels appeared around 800 years ago and were not the sweet, savory, custard-like dish they are today. They were simply a salty dish made only of bread and flour. It was not until the seventeenth century, in Poland, that sugar was introduced to the kugel, and the version we know today came into being.

Alsatian and Bavarian Jews most likely brought this delightful dish to America. It resembled apple pie, as it contained noodle dough and was filled with apples. Eastern European Jewish immigrants then brought their versions of the noodle casserole to America, and it evolved into its modern form. Kugel may be eaten hot or cold, as a meal or a side dish, and is a delicious compliment to any table.

Lox & Smoked Salmon

The word "lox" is derived from the German word *lachs*, meaning salmon. Antiquarians believe it was around 2,000 B.C.E. that the first fish drying and fish smoking station went into operation in Ireland. Since then, salmon and the way it is prepared has undergone surprisingly few changes.

Northern Europeans have long used salt to preserve fish and the tradition has changed little since then. Smokehouses cure the fish in salt, water, and brown sugar before cold-smoking it on racks in ovens containing fruitwood shavings. The salmon farmed in Norway, Chile, the Faeroe Islands (a territory of Denmark), and the wild Pacific salmon from Alaska is processed the same way.

The migration that brought the European immigrants to the United States also brought with them the traditions of smoking and salting fish, but it wasn't until the arrival of the Eastern European Jews in the late nineteenth and early twentieth centuries that the process became popular. Owing to their somewhat limited kitchen facilities, immigrants prized smoked salmon for the

Photo, circa 1960. The matzo-making process at Streit's Matzos is carefully watched over in preparation for Passover. *(Courtesy of Streit's Matzos)*

Photo, circa 1960. A billboard advertising Streit's Salty Moon Matzos. *(Courtesy of Streit's Matzos)*

relative ease of storage and most especially because it was parve and could be eaten with either meat or dairy meals.

"Lox" leapt from the immigrant culture of the Lower East Side to mainstream life and is not really smoked salmon at all. It is actually salmon cured in salt brine with no refrigeration needed. Belly lox is a salty salmon cured in salt brine for months, but not smoked. Nova, the most popular seller today, is salmon cured in a salt-sugar brine for a few days and lightly cold-smoked.

 The genius that married the bagel with cream cheese and lox is a mystery, but we do know that it occurred sometime early in the twentieth century. One possibility is that the famous Jewish entertainer, Al Jolson, who appeared regularly on radio's Kraft musical reviews in the 1930s, might have sung the praises of Kraft cream cheese paired with the bagel and lox on his show. No matter where the union originated, its current popularity — and that of the pink, satiny, heavenly lox alone — is undeniable!

Macaroons

This flourless cookie originated in an Italian monastery around 1792. It is believed that during the French Revolution (1789–99) the Carmelite Nuns baked the cookies to pay for their housing. Italian Jews adopted the recipe and took it with them to Eastern Europe when they were forced to leave Italy. The sweet cookie quickly became a favored dessert.

Macaroons are one of the tastiest cookies and one of the simplest, consisting of egg whites, chopped nuts or shredded coconut, and sugar. Baked to perfection, the macaroon is crunchy on the outside and chewy on the inside. The macaroon is a cookie commonly served for dessert during the Passover holidays and is available at most delis year-round.

Photo, circa 1960. Entertainer Eddie Canter (far left) with wife and friends at a Catskill resort for the Passover week. Note the box of Streit's Matzos on the table. *(Courtesy of Streit's Matzos)*

Product label, circa 1900.
(Courtesy of Rabbi Peter Schweitzer)

Mandelbrot

Mandelbrot is a Yiddish word meaning almond bread, and it describes the Jewish version of Italian biscotti. This twice-baked cookie was supposedly brought to Italy by Spanish Jews who then transported it to Eastern Europe. Another theory is that it came from Poland, through the port of Galveston, and traveled well throughout the western part of the United States. Mandelbrot is ideally served with tea, coffee, or wine.

Matzo

Matzo is basically nothing but flour and water, but oh, what a history this flat bread has to tell! The quick exodus of the Jews from the hands of the pharaoh in Egypt two thousand years ago was the defining moment in the history of the matzo. The fleeing people did not have time to let their bread rise, and so they mixed flour and water together and "baked" it on large, hot rocks as they traveled through the desert to their freedom.

Matzo is prepared swiftly to prevent the water and flour from creating a leavening effect and rising. Only eighteen minutes are allowed from beginning to end, through kneading, rolling, and baking. This is believed to be the exact amount of time it takes water and flour to ferment.

Until the 1840s, Jewish people bought their matzo directly from their synagogues, but matzo bakeries became prevalent in America by the mid-nineteenth century. Before boxed matzos were sold in stores, people bought directly from these bakeries. Now only a few such bakeries exist and most are owned by large corporations. Streit's Matzo is one of the originals — a fourth-generation-run kosher matzo factory still in its original location on Rivington Street in the Lower East Side.

Today, delis serve matzo during Passover, when non-leavened products are eaten exclusively, but it can be found throughout the year in bread baskets and in the form of matzo balls and matzo brie.

Photo, 2004. Hefty matzo balls at Rose's Deli in Portland, Oregon. (Courtesy of Rose's Deli)

Product label, circa 1890. (Courtesy of Rabbi Peter Schweitzer)

Matzo Ball Soup

One of the most contentious foods of all the deli fare is the simple but heavenly chicken soup. Everyone has his or her own opinion about what makes the perfect chicken soup (and the best matzo balls, or *knaydelach* in Yiddish); some prefer matzo balls that are hefty and dense, others prefer them light as a feather.

Truly, a good matzo ball soup is all about the preparation. A basic rich golden chicken soup comes from boiling a whole chicken, adding parsley, a turnip, carrots, onion, and celery. Too much salt . . . not enough salt . . . the complaints do not end, but one thing is for certain — everyone feels comfort after consuming a piping hot bowl of golden broth.

You've heard it a million times: "Jewish Penicillin," and it's true. There are certain anti-inflammatory properties found in the broth from a chicken that help soothe colds, relieve stuffy noses, and cure sore throats. Cystine, an amino acid found in chicken, is chemically similar to a drug prescribed for bronchitis, known as Acetylcystine, which is made from chicken feathers and skin. In the twelfth century, Maimonides, the great rabbi, teacher, and physician, stated in the Mishna Torah

that "soup made from an old chicken is the benefit against chronic fevers . . . and also aids the cough." The healing benefits of a good chicken soup are nothing short of heaven.

The matzo ball is made from ground matzo, or matzo meal, combined with eggs, schmaltz (chicken fat), and seasonings and mixed and rolled into a ball. And herein lies the debate: Is it small, like a Ping-Pong ball, or large, like a tennis ball? And the proportion of matzo meal to eggs decides its fate: light or heavy. Some like "floaters," some like "sinkers"! Any way you have it, it's all in the richness of the chicken broth anyway.

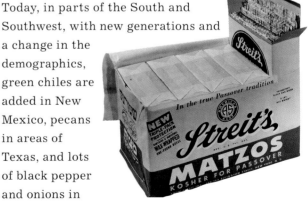

Today, in parts of the South and Southwest, with new generations and a change in the demographics, green chiles are added in New Mexico, pecans in areas of Texas, and lots of black pepper and onions in Louisiana.

Product packaging, circa 1975. (Courtesy of Streit's Matzos)

Pastrami

The pastrami on rye is a hallmark in the deli experience: when you think of deli food, you think of pastrami.

Anywhere in America, the quality of the deli is based on the quality of the pastrami. Pastrami is cured, smoked, and steamed beef navel. The navel, or belly, is the underside of the animal, next to the brisket, and is a much fattier cut, thus making it more tender as it undergoes its process of pickling, spicing, smoking, and steaming. Pastrami has its origins in Turkey, where it was called *basturma*, which means to be pressed. The word evolved into *pastirma* or *postroma* in America, and finally settled into pastrami. This early form of preserved meat was left out to dry in the wind, then was pickled with dried spices, pressed, and sliced. Turkish horsemen pressed the meat flat by placing slabs of it in pockets on the saddle so that the pressure from their legs flattened it as they rode.

Because this type of meat was difficult to make at home, delicatessens stepped in to solve the problem. The processes by which the meat gets to the sandwich vary from deli to deli. One deli steams it for three hours, one for six, another completes the process in two steps. Delis like to claim they make their pastrami from scratch, but in truth, purveyors provide the initial processes of curing, spicing, and smoking the meat. The secret is really in the steaming and how the meat is treated when it finally gets to the individual deli. Also important is slicing the meat against the grain to hold the meat together.

Pickled Herring

Many dishes such as pickled herring or herring in sour cream were not considered Jewish foods in Europe, but they became readily associated with Jewish deli food in the new country. Herring is a very fatty fish found in the open sea as well as in shallow bays near coastal waters. There is a year-round fishing season for herring, which could account for the popularity and diversity of this small fish (the length of a small fork). Herring can be smoked, frozen, pickled with sour cream or served fresh. And this very salty fish is usually served in delis as an appetizer or a side dish.

Photo, circa 1920. The storefront of Gold & Worshowsky Wholesale Butcher shop in New York City.
(Courtesy of Rabbi Peter Schweitzer)

Potato Latkes

Latke is a Yiddish term for a potato pancake that originated in Eastern Europe or Germany around the late eighteenth century. Latkes are oil-fried patties made from grated potatoes, onions, flour, and salt, and you'll find them year-round on every deli menu. They are commonly served as a side dish with applesauce or sour cream.

Latkes are also traditionally eaten on the holiday of Hanukkah, the festival of lights. History tells of when the Maccabees reclaimed their temple from the Syrian Greeks in Jerusalem 2,200 years ago. The oil that remained in their temple's menorah (a symbolic, multibranched candelabrum) was only sufficient to burn for only one day, but, by some miracle, the oil lasted for eight days and eight nights. Today, we eat latkes and other oil-rich foods on this holiday in honor of the oil that lasted beyond its expectancy.

Reuben Sandwich

The Reuben is a grilled sandwich of corned beef, sauerkraut, and Swiss cheese on rye bread. In these modern times, there are newer and possibly lower-fat versions of this sandwich, using turkey and cole slaw, but purists still love the original.

The origins of this sandwich are a bit sketchy, but one thing is for certain: it didn't originate in Eastern Europe. While many did not adhere to kosher food laws, Jews at that time would have never eaten meat and cheese together at the same meal, let alone on a sandwich. The sandwich may have been invented by Reuben Kuklakofsky of Omaha, Nebraska, for one of his poker buddies, who liked it so much he added it to the menu at his Blackstone Hotel. Another version of the Reuben story has it that Arnold Reuben, owner of a few delis in New York City, created this sandwich in 1914 for an actress friend named Annette and then named it for himself.

Postcard, 1953. In its day, Bernstein's Delicatessen was the place to meet in New York City. *(Courtesy of Rabbi Peter Schweitzer)*

Photo, circa 1990. Nothing could be better than a corned beef sandwich and some sour pickles at Canter's Deli in Los Angeles. *(Courtesy of Canter's Deli)*

Rugelach

These crisp, flaky, crescent-shaped pastries are also called butterhorns, horns-of-plenty, cheese bagelach, *kipfel*, or singularly "a little rolled thing." *Rugel* is the Yiddish word for royal, and that name for these cookies is fitting: the taste could bring one to one's knees.

Rugelach, now one of the most familiar cookies served and sold in delis across the country, are thought to have come from Poland, where they were a Hanukkah treat. Butter dough was used for the flaky dough that was then rolled into circles, filled with raisins, nuts, sugar, and cinnamon, and rolled the way a croissant is rolled. In America the dough is usually made rich with cream cheese instead of butter, and the filling may be the traditional raisin, walnut, and cinnamon, chocolate chip, or apricot or prune jam.

Salami, Bologna, and Tongue

The heart of the Jewish deli is the meat — the pastrami, the corned beef, the kosher hot dog, the brisket, and the salami, tongue, and bologna. Delis notoriously give samples of the meats for the customers to try before buying or ordering, and they often sell thick slices by the pound. All the kosher deli meats must adhere to strict regulations of cleanliness and Kashrut. Salami and bologna are cured and seasoned, and the uncooked meats are infused with garlic as the dominant spice.

Tongue is deli meat prized by many. Its flavor can be smoked or pickled; salty and smoked; or gingery, sweet, and pickled depending on the spicing, which, besides the garlic, can include ginger, bay leaves, paprika, nutmeg, and brown sugar. The meat is then boiled, sliced thin, and served hot or cold for sandwiches or as entrées. Another popular method involves baking the tongue with tomato, or a sweet and sour sauce with garlic, and served hot. The name tongue may be a little off-putting, but it really is a treat.

Salt

As it is said in the Talmud, "The world can get along without pepper, but it cannot get along without salt." Salt is significant in Jewish life. In ancient times, treaties were sealed with salt. It is traditional to bring salt, along with sugar, flour, and bread, to a new home so that the family will always have the four most basic ingredients to prepare a meal.

The use of kosher salt is important in the preparation of meat for the kosher table. Kosher salt is used to soak and salt the meat to remove the final traces of blood thus rendering the meat kosher. Its large coarse grains have a wider surface area, which allows for greater absorption. With no additives, kosher salt is nutritionally no different from regular table salt, but the flavor is somewhat more definitive.

Schmaltz

The reason that *schmaltz* is still around is probably pure nostalgia. This rendered fat from a chicken or goose evokes a trip down memory lane for people of a certain age, and it was once considered a symbol of abundance in Jewish cooking. There's a Yiddish saying: "He's so lucky that even when he falls, he falls right into a schmaltz bucket!"

In Europe rendered chicken or goose fat is clarified and cooled and used as a spread for bread. It is also used in potato pancakes or in chopped liver to en-hance the flavor. In America it is still used by many who prize the flavor and don't worry about the fat content. For them, it is like butter! They spread hard schmaltz on bread and pour soft schmaltz like melted butter on chicken livers or in egg salad.

The word *schmaltz* is a Yiddish word, used to describe anything that is overly sentimental. Just don't get too schmaltzy!

Flyer, 1985. Add seltzer to this syrup and milk for the perfect egg cream. *(Courtesy of Fox's u-bet Syrup)*

Photo, 2003. Stopping for a treat and some friendly conversation at Russ & Daughters Appetizing Store in New York City.

Photo, 2005. *(Courtesy of Rose's Deli)*

Seltzer

Fresh spring water — or tea water, as it was called — was sold from horse-drawn carts around the 1790s in New York City. By 1809 a process was developed to carbonate the water and the seltzer craze in America began. "Two cents plain," or Jewish champagne, described a glass of cold seltzer water in America in the early 1900s. This effervescent, nonalcoholic beverage was a perfect complement to rich deli foods. It was sometimes even referred to as "belchwasser," or burp water. And no true egg cream would be right without that spritz of fresh seltzer water.

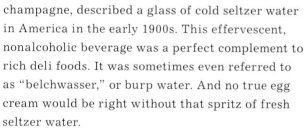

Seltzer was made from purified water filtered through charcoal and paper to remove all traces of salt. Then carbon dioxide was pumped into the glass bottle under high pressure, capped, and, if you were lucky, it was delivered to your home in beautiful green and blue glass bottles.

Tzimmes

Tzimmes (pronounced *tsi-mes*) is a Yiddish word for a sweet, culinary side dish made variously of stewed carrots, honey, raisins, and prunes. There is tzimmes with meat and tzimmes without meat, and it can be spiced with cinnamon, paprika, honey, or orange juice.

The origins of this unusual dish come from Germany, where there was a tradition of cooking fruit with meat. The word *tzimmes* is derived from the Middle High German word *zuomuose*, which refers to any side dish. As Ashkenazi Jews moved eastward to Poland and began speaking Yiddish, pronunciation of the word evolved into tzimmes, which, in Yiddish, means "to make a big fuss." *Gantze tzimmes* means to make an even greater fuss!

Tzimmes is considered the perfect complement to the main course of a Jewish feast. It is traditionally served on Rosh Hashanah to bring in a new and sweet year, but you don't have to wait for a holiday to enjoy this tasty side dish. It is served in delis year-round.

DELI 101
YIDDISHISMS AND DELI-SPEAK
Part III

Photo, circa 1960. It takes a number of rabbis to bless the matzo as it is made for Passover.
(Courtesy of Streit's Matzos)

Photo, circa 1930. An exterior of the Streit's Matzo bakery on the Lower East Side of New York City.
(Courtesy of Streit's Matzos)

Although not a national language, Yiddish is spoken by Jews around the world. Yiddish is a blend of various German dialects that emerged from out of the Jewish ghettos of Central Europe around 1100 C.E. Before long, the language traveled the world, providing a sense of unity among the Jews of the Diaspora (the scattering of Jews into other regions after leaving Palestine). Over time, Yiddish expanded from its roots as a collection of Germanic dialects to a language that incorporated elements of Hebrew, Aramaic, Slavic, and the Romance languages. Eastern European immigrants commonly spoke Yiddish when they arrived in America, allowing for communication and encouraging community among people of various ethnic origins. Yiddish uses Hebrew characters and, as with Hebrew, is written from right to left. It is not be confused with Hebrew, however. It sounds more like a Germanic language, with its hard consonants and sometimes guttural inflections, than it does a language from a region of the Middle East.

Although fewer and fewer people are able to read or even fluently speak Yiddish, its phrases have made their way into common usage, and some have even been recorded in American dictionaries. These include a long list of insults, innuendoes, and, of course, food references.

Page 60: Photo, 1960. A busy lunchtime at Stage Deli in New York City.

Yiddishisms

a bisel: *a little*

babka: *coffee cake-style pastry*

balabusta: *a term to represent an efficient Jewish homemaker*

batempte: *tasty, delicious*

borscht: *beet soup*

Borscht Belt: *an informal term for the summer resorts of the Catskill Mountains, frequented by Jewish New Yorkers in the 1940s through the 1960s*

chrain: *horseradish*

es gezunterhait: *eat in good health*

ess: *eat*

forshpeiz: *appetizer*

fressen: *to overeat, devour*

geshmak: *tasty, delicious*

greps: *a mild burp*

hak flaish: *chopped meat*

holishes: *stuffed cabbage*

kasha: *groats, mush cereal, buckwheat, porridge; a mess, mix-up, confusion*

kasha varnishkes: *cooked groats and bow-tie noodles*

kibbitz: *to joke and make wisecracks*

kiddish: *blessing over the wine on the eve of Sabbath or festivals*

kishkeh: *stuffed derma; sausage shaped, stuffed with a mixture of flour, onions, salt, pepper, and schmaltz to keep it together, then boiled, roasted, and sliced*

knaidel: *dumplings, or matzo balls, usually made of matzo meal and cooked in soup*

knishes: *baked dough pockets filled with potato, meat, or vegetables*

kosher: *Jewish dietary laws based on the cleanliness of certain foods and their preparations*

kreplach: *small pockets of dough filled with chopped meat; eaten in soup or fried*

kugel: *noodle pudding*

lokshen: *noodles*

maven: *expert, connoisseur, authority*

nit kosher: *impure food*

nosh: *to eat a little something*

nosherie: *snack food*

plats: *to burst; bust your guts out; split your guts*

ptsha: *cow's feet in jelly*

pupiklech: *dish of chicken gizzards*

schmaltz: *grease or rendered chicken or goose fat*

schmeer: *to spread*

schnapps: *booze*

schnecken: *small fruit and nut coffee rolls*

schtikel: *small bit or piece; a morsel*

strudel: *sweet cake made of rolled up paper-thin dough*

taiglech: *small pieces of baked dough or small cakes dipped in honey*

tam: *flavor*

trefe: *forbidden food, impure, contrary to the Jewish dietary laws, non-kosher*

tzimmes: *a fruit and/or vegetable stew*

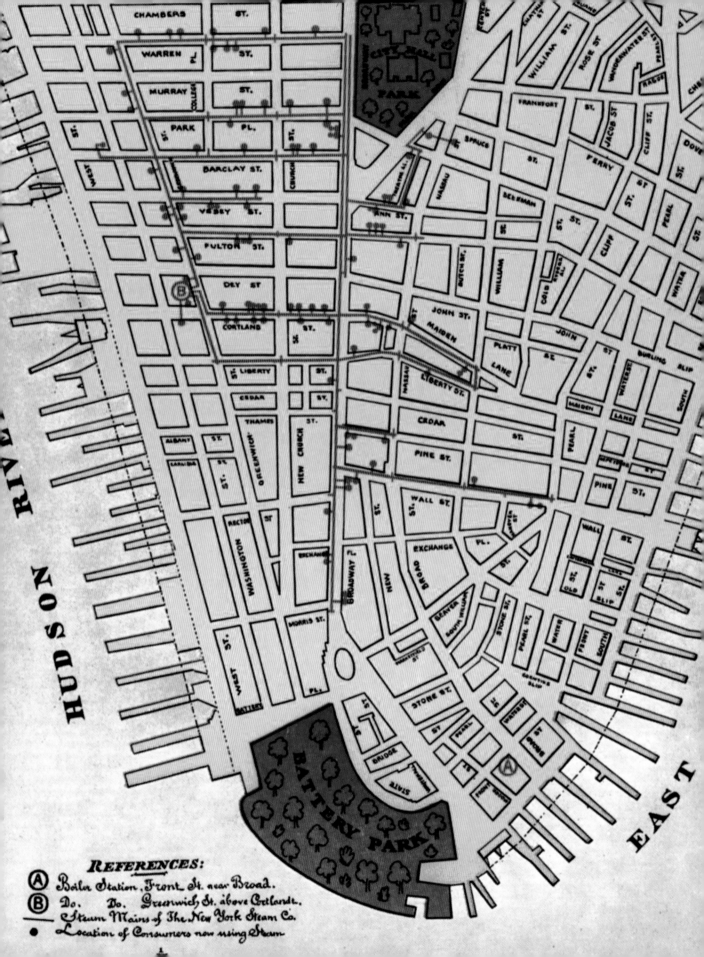

Photo, circa 1925. Elihu Mazo's grocery store on King Street in Charleston, South Carolina. Pictured, left to right (back row): A. J. Novitt, Mr. Feldstein, Florence Mazo, Anastasia Mazo, Nettie Soloman, Elihu Mazo; (front row) Donald Mazo, Norma Mazo, Miriam Soloman. Early Jewish grocery stores were often referred to as local delis, and many evolved into delicatessens as time passed. Sadly, many of the delis in the South have long since closed. *(Courtesy of Harriet Spanier; Special Collections, College of Charleston Library, Charleston, South Carolina)*

Deli-Speak

Delis have contributed to the language of the short-order cook. "Deli-speak" may even be a whole new language!

21 or 211: *two items on one plate*
Adam's ale: *water*
baby: *glass of milk*
break it and shake it: *any egg in a drink*
burn: *a chocolate milk shake*
burn it and let it swim: *a float*
CB: *corned beef*
CB dress: *corned beef with coleslaw and Russian dressing*
clean up the kitchen: *hamburger or hash*
combination: *any sandwich with two meats*
combo: *ham and Swiss*
double L: *rolled beef*
Dutch: *anything with American cheese*
eighty-seven and a half: *attractive female approaching*

first lady: *spareribs*
grade A: *a glass of milk*
in the hay: *strawberry milkshake*
jack: *American cheese and tomato*
jackhammer: *American cheese, tomato, and ham*
make it virtue: *cherry-flavored Coke*
nervous pudding: *gelatin*
one off: *plain frankfurter*
one with: *frankfurter with sauerkraut*
pistol: *pastrami*
RB combo: *roast beef and Swiss cheese*
regular: *coffee with milk and sugar*
schmeer: *a spread of cream cheese on a bagel*
twist it, crack it, and make it crackle: *chocolate malt with a raw egg in it*
whiskey down: *toasted rye bread*
wing-ding setup: *plastic cup with ice*

BEHIND THE COUNTER
POPULAR DELIS AND RECIPES
Part IV

Logo, 2000. This is the same logo 2nd Avenue Deli has been using since it opened in the early 1950s. *(Courtesy of 2nd Avenue Deli)*

Photo, circa 1970. Morris Gottesman and 2nd Avenue Deli's founder, Abe Lebewohl. *(Courtesy of 2nd Avenue Deli)*

Photo, circa 1960. One of the many successful catering events that Abe Lebewohl enjoyed. *(Courtesy of 2nd Avenue Deli)*

2nd Avenue Deli

When Jewish immigrants from Eastern Europe first came to New York City, they were usually too poor to eat out, but when they began venturing out in search of a home away from home, 2nd Avenue Deli was there for them. Jewish humorist Sam Levenson wrote about this adored deli some years ago, remembering how things used to be and how many of these same hospitalities still remain the same.

It all started in 1954, when Polish immigrant Abe Lebewohl took over a ten-seat diner on the corner of 2nd Avenue and Tenth Street in New York City. Abe, who had emigrated from Poland in 1939, started as a soda jerk, and went on to create what would ultimately become one of the most famous and well-respected kosher delis in America. Abe developed the recipes, catered to the customers as if they were family, and was a pillar in the community.

When Abe died tragically in 1996, the world mourned a gentle and enduring man. But his legend remains. Little has changed in this delicatessen in the last half century. The menu is basically the same as it has always been. Here one can enjoy not only deli fare, but a full meal of boiled beef flanken, a mixed platter of meatballs, kishka and stuffed cabbage, or the famous traditional chicken in the pot, made with noodles, carrots, and matzo balls.

On September 11, 2001, 2nd Avenue Deli was there for the very reason that delis existed in the first place. It fed the throngs of people streaming in dazed and frightened, fed the firefighters and other rescuers, and fed the neighborhood when no one knew what to do or where to go. If you lived in the neighborhood, you had a home. And with Jewish holidays coming only a week later, 2nd Avenue Deli was under considerable hardship due to the difficulty of filling deliveries, yet it still managed to honor all its hundreds of holiday orders.

Although the deli moved locations in 2006, the original 2nd Avenue Deli was all about history, nostalgia, and a remembrance of things past. Movies were made there, celebrities ate there, and there was a Hollywood-like walk of fame outside honoring beloved Yiddish actors who once frequented this historic neighborhood (which remains a tourist stop even though the deli has a new home on East 33rd Street). It may not be on 2nd Avenue anymore, but to the loyal fans of this venerable delicatessen, things will never change.

Page 66: Photo, 2003. The landmark Russ & Daughters Appetizing Store on Houston Street in New York City. Its gleaming deli cases are brimming with delicate smoked salmon, herring, pickled lox, and salads.

Postcard, circa 1890. Emigrant landing in New York City.
(Courtesy of Rabbi Peter Schweitzer)

Postcard, circa 1890. A perfect view of the Statue of Liberty as seen from the ships that brought immigrants to America.
(Courtesy of Rabbi Peter Schweitzer)

2nd Avenue Deli
Chopped Liver

1 1/2 pounds beef liver

1 pound chicken liver

Corn oil for drizzling

2 tablespoons plus 2 teaspoons corn oil

1 tablespoon plus 2 teaspoons
   schmaltz (chicken fat)

4 (4 cups) yellow onions, coarsely chopped

4 hard-boiled eggs, peeled

2 teaspoons salt

1/4 teaspoon pepper

Heat broiler.

Rinse the beef and chicken livers thoroughly, and cut away the membranes and extra fat. Cut the beef liver into 1-inch pieces; chicken livers can remain whole. Place beef and chicken livers in a large baking pan, and drizzle with corn oil. (Pour oil into a flatware tablespoon and drizzle over livers; 2 tablespoons are ample.) Broil 8 to 10 minutes. (Keep an eye on it to make sure it doesn't burn.)

Turn liver pieces, and broil for another 5 minutes. Liver should be fully cooked and lightly browned on both sides. Let it chill in the refrigerator.

In a large skillet, heat corn oil and 1 tablespoon of the schmaltz. Add the onions and sauté until well browned. Place in the refrigerator to chill. Meanwhile, in the bowl of a food processor fitted with a metal blade, combine the liver, onions, hard-boiled eggs, remaining schmaltz, salt, and pepper, and blend until smooth. You'll have to do it in batches. Chill before serving.

Serves 8

Note: Chicken livers may be used for a lighter, creamier chopped liver.

2nd Avenue Deli
Chicken Soup

12 cups cold water

1 pound chicken parts

2 stalks celery, including leafy tops,
   cut into 3-inch pieces

1 whole chicken, thoroughly rinsed

Salt to rub inside chicken

1 large, firm yellow onion, unpeeled

1 large carrot, peeled

1 parsnip, peeled

2 teaspoons salt, plus more as needed

1/4 teaspoon pepper, plus more as needed

1 bunch dill, cleaned and tied with a string

Cooked noodles, rice, kasha, or matzo balls (optional)

Pour the water into a large stockpot and add the chicken parts and celery. Bring to a boil. While water is heating, rub the inside of the chicken with salt.

Add the chicken to the pot, cover, reduce heat, and simmer for 30 minutes. Test whole chicken with a fork to see if it's tender and fully cooked. Remove it from the pot and set aside on a large platter. Leave chicken parts in the pot. Add onion, carrot, parsnip, salt, and pepper. Simmer for 1 hour and 15 minutes.

When the chicken cools, remove skin and bones and cut into bite-sized pieces. You can add it to the soup, just before serving, or save it for chicken salad. Strain the soup, and discard everything solid except the carrot. Add dill for 1 minute just before serving and remove and discard. Add salt and pepper to taste. Slice cooked carrot and toss into soup. Add chicken pieces if desired, and noodles, rice, kasha, or matzo balls, if using.

Serves 8

Note: The deli's recipe calls for a whole chicken plus 1 pound of chicken parts. If preferred, you can use 1 large chicken and cut off wings, neck, and one leg to use as parts.

2nd Avenue Deli Matzo Balls

4 large eggs

1/3 cup schmaltz (chicken fat)

1 tablespoon plus 1/4 teaspoon salt

1/4 teaspoon pepper

1 tablespoon baking powder

1 1/3 cups matzo meal

Crack the eggs into a large bowl and beat thoroughly. Beat in schmaltz, 1/4 teaspoon salt, pepper, and baking powder. Slowly fold in matzo meal, mixing vigorously until completely blended. Refrigerate for 30 minutes.

Fill a large stockpot 3/4 full of water, add the 1 tablespoon salt, and bring to a rapid boil. Wet your hands, and, folding the mixture in your palms, shape perfect balls about 1 1/4 inches in diameter. (They will double in size when cooked.) Gently place the matzo balls in the boiling water, and reduce heat to a simmer. Cook for 25 minutes. Remove with a slotted spoon and place 1 or 2 in each bowl of soup. Serve immediately.

Makes 12 to 14 balls

Photo, circa 1983. Actor Milton Berle celebrates the opening of his off-Broadway play, *Goodnight Grandpa*, with Abe Lebewohl and friends at 2nd Avenue Deli. *(Courtesy of 2nd Avenue Deli)*

Below: Menu, 2004. A reproduction of the original 2nd Avenue Deli menu — with original prices — in celebration of the deli's 50th anniversary. *(Courtesy of 2nd Avenue Deli)*

2ND AVE DELI

KOSHER RESTAURANT AND CATERERS

Abe Lebewohl · 1931 - 1996

50th Anniversary

ORIGINAL DELI MENU

PRICES ROLLED BACK TO ORIGINAL MENU PRICES!*

2nd Avenue Deli · 50th Anniversary

SINCE 1954

ORIGINAL DELI MENU

PRICES ROLLED BACK TO ORIGINAL MENU PRICES!*

Appetizers

Chicken Fricassee	.40	Derma	.40
Chopped Liver	.40	Meat Ball	.50

Soups

Pea Soup	.20	Matzo Ball	.40
Kasha, Noodle or Rice	.20		

Entrees

*All entrees served with potato and vegetable

Hungarian Goulash	1.25	Boiled Chicken	1.25
Chicken Fricassee	1.00	Breast of Beef	1.25
Meat Balls	1.00	Liver Steak	1.25
Meat Loaf	1.00	Chopped Steak	1.25
Pepper Steak	1.25	Roast Turkey	1.45
Roast Chicken	1.25	2 Specials	1.15

Sandwiches

*On rye, club 10 extra

Meat Ball	.50	Chopped Liver	.50
Corned Beef	.50	Turkey	.50
Breast of Beef	.50	Roast Beef	.50
Pastrami	.50	Frankfurter on Roll	.15
Salami	.35	Egg Salad	.35
Bologna	.35	Chicken Salad	.35
Tuna Fish	.35	Lettuce & Tomato	.15

Side Orders

Potato Salad	.20	French Fried Potatoes	.20
Cole Slaw	.20	Square Potato Knishes	.10

Desserts

Cookies	.15	Marble Cake	.15
Jello	.15		

Beverages

Fountain Sodas	.15	Coffee or Tea	.05

*Served on premises only, from 11:30 AM to 8:00 PM. No delivery, takeout or doggie bags.

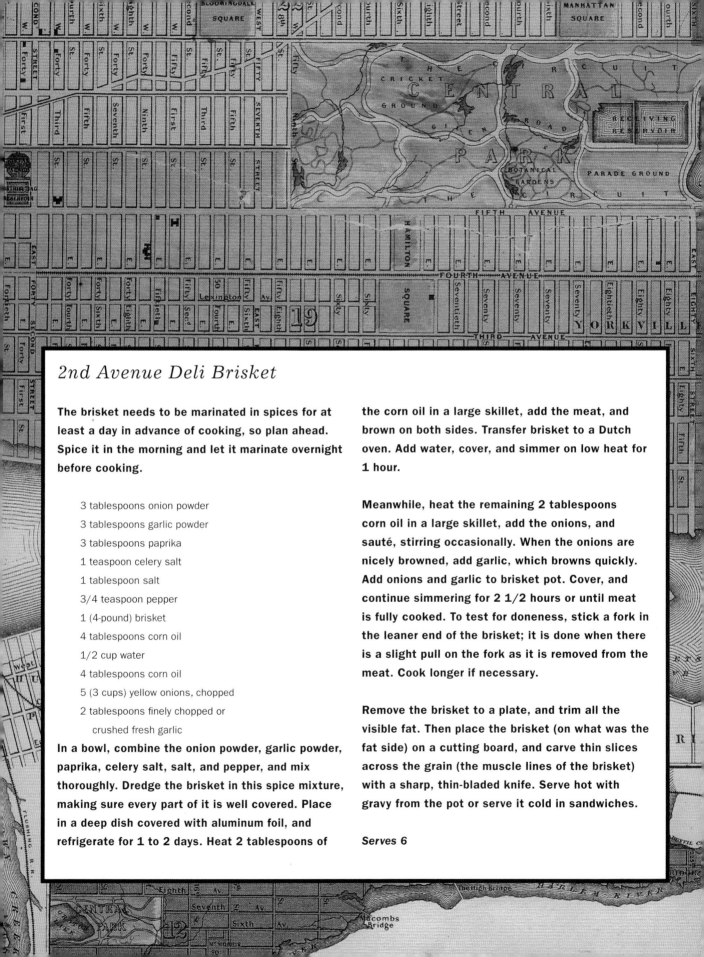

2nd Avenue Deli Brisket

The brisket needs to be marinated in spices for at least a day in advance of cooking, so plan ahead. Spice it in the morning and let it marinate overnight before cooking.

3 tablespoons onion powder

3 tablespoons garlic powder

3 tablespoons paprika

1 teaspoon celery salt

1 tablespoon salt

3/4 teaspoon pepper

1 (4-pound) brisket

4 tablespoons corn oil

1/2 cup water

4 tablespoons corn oil

5 (3 cups) yellow onions, chopped

2 tablespoons finely chopped or crushed fresh garlic

In a bowl, combine the onion powder, garlic powder, paprika, celery salt, salt, and pepper, and mix thoroughly. Dredge the brisket in this spice mixture, making sure every part of it is well covered. Place in a deep dish covered with aluminum foil, and refrigerate for 1 to 2 days. Heat 2 tablespoons of the corn oil in a large skillet, add the meat, and brown on both sides. Transfer brisket to a Dutch oven. Add water, cover, and simmer on low heat for 1 hour.

Meanwhile, heat the remaining 2 tablespoons corn oil in a large skillet, add the onions, and sauté, stirring occasionally. When the onions are nicely browned, add garlic, which browns quickly. Add onions and garlic to brisket pot. Cover, and continue simmering for 2 1/2 hours or until meat is fully cooked. To test for doneness, stick a fork in the leaner end of the brisket; it is done when there is a slight pull on the fork as it is removed from the meat. Cook longer if necessary.

Remove the brisket to a plate, and trim all the visible fat. Then place the brisket (on what was the fat side) on a cutting board, and carve thin slices across the grain (the muscle lines of the brisket) with a sharp, thin-bladed knife. Serve hot with gravy from the pot or serve it cold in sandwiches.

Serves 6

2nd Avenue Deli
Stuffed Cabbage

Stuffing:

1 1/2 pounds chopped meat

3/4 cup uncooked white rice

1 (1 cup) yellow onion finely chopped

2 eggs, beaten

1/2 cup water

1 (1 tablespoon) garlic clove, finely chopped or crushed

2 teaspoons salt

1/2 teaspoon pepper

Sauce:

2 cups tomato sauce

1 1/2 cups finely chopped yellow onions

1/2 orange, chopped with peel into 1/2-inch
   pieces and seeded

2/3 lemon, chopped with peel into 1/2-inch
    pieces and seeded

1/2 teaspoon ground cinnamon

1 cup granulated sugar

1/2 cup brown sugar

1/2 cup white vinegar

2 cups water

1 1/2 teaspoons salt

1 large lightweight young green cabbage

1 small to medium green cabbage

4 cups cabbage, chopped into 3/4-inch pieces
   (use cabbage for stuffing, leaves removed)

In a bowl, combine the ingredients for the stuffing. Stir them with a fork, and then mix thoroughly with your hands. Cover and refrigerate. In another bowl, thoroughly mix all sauce ingredients except cabbage. Cover and refrigerate.

Fill a very large stockpot 3/4 full with water and bring to a rapid boil. Using a thin, sharp knife, make deep cuts around the core of the large cabbage. (Cut into the cabbage in a circle about 1/4-inch out from the core.) Lift out the core, making a hole about 2 inches wide and 2 1/2 inches deep.

This is a bit difficult; persevere. Set out a baking tray near the stove. Stick a long cooking fork into the core hole of the large cabbage, and plunge it (carefully so you don't splash yourself) into the pot of rapidly boiling water. The outer leaves will begin to fall off. Leave them in the boiling water for a few minutes until they're limp and flexible enough for stuffing, then take them out one at a time and place them on the baking tray. Try not to tear the leaves. When all the leaves are on the tray, transfer it into the sink and pour the boiling water from the pot over the leaves. Wash the leaves carefully in cold water. With a small, sharp knife trim off the tough outer spines and discard them.

Find your largest leaves, and set them out on a plate. Set out all other leaves on another plate. One at a time, line each large leaf with another large leaf or two smaller leaves. (The idea is to strengthen your cabbage wrapping, so that the stuffing stays securely inside during cooking. Be sure to align the spines of inner and outer leaves.) Stuff with 3/4 cup of the meat/rice mixture. Roll very tightly along the spine, and close both sides by tucking them in with your fingers. The spine should be vertical in the center of your roll. Stir the 4 cups of chopped cabbage into the sauce. Pour sauce about 3/4 of an inch into a large, wide-bottomed stockpot. Arrange the cabbage rolls carefully on top of the sauce, and pour the remaining sauce over them to cover. Cover the pot and simmer for 1 hour and 45 minutes.

Serves 3 to 4 (7 rolls)

Note: When you're confronted with a bin of cabbages, you'll notice that some are quite light, while others have the heft of bowling balls. Choose the lightest ones for stuffing; their leaves peel off much more easily.

Photo, 1990. Seymour Attman, son of founders,
Harry and Ida, at the entrance of his family's deli.
(Courtesy of Attman's)

Attman's

The story of Attman's in Baltimore, Maryland, is that of the classic, multigenerational, family-owned business. Attman's went from being a place where herring and pickles were sold from barrels in front of the small deli to becoming a legend on Baltimore's "corned beef row." (At one time, more corned beef was sold in East Baltimore than anywhere else in the United States.) In its early days, corned beef row was a thriving marketplace, something like a giant delicatessen, with fish mongers, bakeries, pushcarts, and fruit stands lining the streets. There were horseradish grinders and dairy and poultry shops. You could find bagels, smoked fish, and live chickens. Herring was sold from wooden barrels and wrapped in newspaper, a custom long since lost.

In the late nineteenth and early twentieth centuries, immigrants from Eastern Europe settled in the eastern section of Baltimore and, as with all large populations of émigrés, they set about making a living the best way that they knew how. Russian immigrants Harry and Ida Attman began with a small deli on East Baltimore Street in 1915, and in 1927 the deli moved to its present location on Lombard Street. The Attmans raised their family in this very colorful era when the sights, sounds, smells, and tastes evoked nostalgia for the days of yesteryear. Their son, Seymour, began working at a young age, and continued to operate Attman's throughout his life. He became a beloved and respected member of the community as well as one of the most admired philanthropists in Baltimore. In 1968, he enlarged the deli with a "kibbitz" room, in memory of his son, Stuart.

In the beginning, there were no tables or chairs at Attman's, just one long counter that gave the businessmen who frequented the deli a place to eat standing up. Sawdust, which kept the floor clean, was replaced each night. In the early twentieth century most delis were merely grocery stores with barrels of spices, nuts, and various types of herring. There was never a formal menu; the customers read from a menu board behind the counter. Selling sandwiches was primarily a way to lure business into the store, where corned beef sandwiches were sold for a nickel. But that eventually changed, and the deli was expanded to full-service, including all the traditional deli foods — matzo ball soup, knishes, kugels, and smoked fish.

Attman's became the envy of the southeastern part of the United States, where there was a huge absence of Jewish grocery stores and delis. Throughout the South, the northern deli filled orders for corned beef, knishes, breads, smoked fish, and seasonal Jewish foods that were in demand for the Jewish holidays as well as throughout the year.

In time, the neighborhood changed and many of the businesses moved away or closed their doors. But Attman's is still there, a valiant survivor —

vintage Baltimore! Under the stewardship of Marc Attman, grandson of Harry Attman, the deli makes its own salami, bologna, and knishes, and the bread pudding here is divine. Once referred to as Baltimore's United Nations, everyone came here, from the average working person to dignitaries, from professional athletes to senators, governors, and mayors. Even President Jimmy Carter came here for a classic Baltimore-style kosher hot dog — wrapped with grilled bologna. Strictly a Baltimore tradition!

Photo, 1975. Seymour Attman stands beside the menu board celebrating the deli's 60th anniversary. *(Courtesy of Attman's)*

Attman's Bread Pudding

1 1/2 pounds (1 1/2 loaves) egg bread, cubed

4 cups granulated sugar

1/2 cup brown sugar

1 tablespoon ground ginger

1 tablespoon ground cinnamon

24 eggs

1 quart half-and-half

2 tablespoons pure vanilla extract

1 stick butter, melted

Preheat the oven to 350 degrees. Grease a 16 x 13-inch baking pan. Combine all the dry ingredients in a large bowl. Mix the wet ingredients together in a separate large bowl. Add the dry ingredients to the wet ingredients and mix well. Bake, uncovered, for 20 minutes, or until golden. Serve it warm or cold as a side dish or entrée.

Serves 14 to 16

Postcard, circa 1890. A market on Hester Street in New York City. *(Courtesy of Rabbi Peter Schweitzer)*

Opposite page: Photo, 1939. Attman's place on the famed "corned beef row" (aka Lombard Street) in East Baltimore. *(Courtesy of The Baltimore Sun)*

Attman's Noodle Kugel

1 pound cream cheese, at room temperature

1 cup sour cream

2 cups (4 sticks) butter

6 eggs

1 cup sugar

2 pints half-and-half

1 teaspoon pure vanilla extract

1 1/4 pound cooked wide egg noodles

Crumb topping:

4 cups cornflakes

1 cup brown sugar

1/4 cup (2 sticks) butter, melted

Preheat the oven to 350 degrees. Grease a 9 x 12 x 4-inch-deep pan. Combine the cream cheese, sour cream, butter, eggs, and sugar. Add the half-and-half and vanilla extract, mix well, and then mix in the egg noodles. Pour the ingredients in a baking dish. In a separate bowl, combine the cornflakes, sugar, and butter. Mix and spread the topping onto the kugel. Cover with aluminum foil and bake for 25 minutes. Remove the foil and bake for an additional 10 minutes, or until it is golden on top.

Serves 6 to 8

Attman's Reuben Dip

2 pounds corned beef, chopped

1 pound shredded Swiss cheese

1/2 cup ketchup

4 tablespoons mustard

1/2 cup chopped yellow onions

1/2 cup sweet pickle relish

1 pound cream cheese, at room temperature

1 cup sour cream

1 12-inch round Russian rye bread, for serving

1 loaf rye bread, cubed, for serving

Place the beef, Swiss cheese, ketchup, mustard, onions, relish, cream cheese, and sour cream in a large bowl and stir to combine well. Cut the top off of a round Russian rye bread. Scoop out the inside of bread. Add dip to hollowed-out bread and serve with the cubed rye bread. Refrigerate until it is served.

Serves 4

Barney Greengrass

Barney Greengrass, known for decades as The Sturgeon King, apprenticed on the Lower East Side of New York before opening his own appetizing store in 1908 in Harlem. Two decades later, he moved his business to Amsterdam Avenue on the Upper West Side of Manhattan. It looks today like it did in 1929. Why fool with success? The original Formica tables and the peeling wallpaper are part of the charm, but the reason to come here is the food. Heaping platters of lox, bagels, smoked fish, and scrambled eggs with lox and onions are what keep people lining up outside.

In this neighborhood deli you'll taste some of the best smoked fish around. There is a feel here of what a deli used to be like. On rainy days, to keep the floors clean, grandson Gary sprinkles sawdust on the floors — a nostalgic touch. There is a sense of community, and no one really needs a menu; customers know what they can expect and they rely on it. The regulars run a tab.

The deli, which is named for its founder, sits on what were formerly tracts of farmland and country estates known as Bloomingdale Village. Barney Greengrass sits on what was once the 200-acre farm owned by

Edgar Allen Poe and his wife, who moved there to escape what they described as the insufferably dirty streets of New York City. This formerly pastoral, rural setting is now a bustling, noisy, and vibrant part of New York City.

Among other things, Barney Greengrass has been a well-known celebrity hangout for decades. Groucho Marx, Al Jolson, Irving Berlin, Danny Kaye, Zero Mostel, and authors Arthur Miller and Isaac Bashevis Singer were regulars. Phillip Roth, Harvey Keitel, and Paul Reiser are current regulars, lending a flavor of "old New York."

The menu at Barney Greengrass reads like a tribute to all mouthwatering deli foods, each with a description of its history and preparation. The sturgeon, the filet mignon of fish, is smoked to a flawless end and hand-sliced. The heavenly eastern Nova Scotia salmon, the deli's most popular fish, is wood-smoked, mild, and salty. The western Nova Scotia salmon is leaner, saltier, and a luscious red color. These Pacific salmon are cured, smoked, and hand-sliced for a not-to-be-forgotten experience. The salty lox, which is standard fare, is usually ordered by the novice, and is as salty, silky, and smoky as the others. The whitefish is hickory-smoked; and the chubs, baby whitefish, sable, and codfish fillets are smoked, infused with garlic, and spiced with paprika. There is kippered salmon; rainbow brook trout; pastrami salmon sprinkled with a peppercorn spread; gravlax cured with dill, white peppercorns, and a splash of vodka; homemade borscht; smoky whitefish salad; and pickled lox. This is but a small sampling of the delicious delicacies at this authentic Old World eatery. You could order meat here, but why would you want to? Meat is only five percent of the business. The bulk of the business is in the silky smoked fishes that look as though they had just jumped off the boat.

Celebrities have long called Barney Greengrass their second home, and films and television shows have been filmed in or around the deli. While filming a scene for the series "Law and Order," director James Frawley told the story that it was his grandfather who long ago coined the moniker "The Sturgeon King."

As with all multigenerational family-run businesses, the stories abound. Groucho Marx once said, "Barney Greengrass may not have ruled any kingdoms or written any great symphonies, but he did a monumental job with sturgeon." You could order in or out, as in the 1940s when an order was sent to FDR; Barney Greengrass used to say on his mailing labels, "If it's not delivered in three days, never mind."

Barney's son, Moe Greengrass, a beloved figure in the neighborhood, used to slice salmon with the skill of a surgeon, never scrimping and always making sure the customer was entertained by his magic tricks behind the counter as well as in front of it.

Few delis like this exist anymore; many have been updated or modernized. Here it's just like it was seventy-five years ago. And as Gary Greengrass says, "It's a comfortable shoe."

Barney Greengrass Cheese Blintzes

Crêpes:
4 eggs
3 cups all-purpose flour
4 cups milk
butter

Filling:
3 pounds farmer cheese
4 eggs, plus 1 beaten egg
1 cup sugar
1 teaspoon water
Sour cream, for garnish
Applesauce, for garnish

To make the crêpes, whisk all the ingredients together in a bowl. Place in the refrigerator for 1 1/2 hours to chill completely.

Heat some butter in a frying pan over medium heat. Drop 2 tablespoons of the batter into the pan. Tilt the pan to coat with the batter, cook through, about 1 minute or until the crêpe pulls away from the side, and remove the crêpe with a flat spatula. Stack on a plate, cooked side down. Repeat until all the batter is used.

To make the filling, combine the farmer cheese, 4 of the eggs, and the sugar together in a large bowl. Place 3 tablespoons of the cheese mixture onto the crêpe and fold over. Add water to the 1 beaten egg and use the mixture to close the blintz. Heat some butter in a skillet, and fry on both sides until the crêpe is brown. Serve it warm with sour cream or applesauce on the side.

Serves 10 to 12 (35 blintzes)

"Only Life Offers More Variety!"

Ben's Kosher Delicatessen

Ben's Kosher Delicatessen is a come-from-behind success story and is a tribute to hard work and determination. A boy from humble beginnings in the 1960s, Ronnie Dragoon had a dream and saw it to fruition. After college, he opened his first deli in Baldwin, New York, and soon, others followed. But the one that is an institution is the one in Manhattan on West 38th Street; that was once the site of the former Lou G. Siegel's Restaurant and Deli. Siegel's opened in 1917 and was a venerable old deli and longstanding kosher meat restaurant that offered real Jewish food. It was the place for special occasions, parties, and reunions. Rudy Vallee and Harry Ritz of the Ritz Brothers often dined on their flanken in a pot. At that time, Lou G. Siegel's baked its own breads and pastries and cured its own meats. When the deli was sold to Ronnie Dragoon and it became Ben's, it was a trophy in the hands of the new owners, and a springboard for more delis to come.

Manhattan is a city of neighborhoods, and Ben's Kosher Delicatessen fills the need that the older Lou G. Siegel's filled for so many years — a deli in the heart of the Garment District, which is a sure thing when it comes to having built-in clientele. Men and women who had offices nearby congregated daily for their kosher meals, and they still do! Some added attractions are Ben's signature coleslaw and kishka and its fabulous chicken in the pot.

Since 1998 a distinguishing event has occurred annually at Ben's — the Annual Charity Matzo Ball Eating Contest, with proceeds donated to the Interfaith Nutrition Network. Every January, at the 38th Street location, contestants must consume as many baseball-sized matzo balls as they are able in the allotted time of five minutes and 25 seconds. The grand prize is a gift certificate and the sought-after Matzo Ball Trophy. This contest has become an event not to miss in New York City. And so has Ben's.

BEN'S
NY KOSHER

BUY-ONE-GET-ONE FREE!!!

Promotional card, 2004. *(Courtesy of Ben's Kosher Delicatessen and Paul Warchol Photography)*

Postcard, circa 1890. A Lower East Side street scene, New York City. *(Courtesy of Rabbi Peter Schweitzer)*

Ben's Kosher Delicatessen Noodle Kugel

1 pound wide egg noodles
10 extra-large eggs
2 (15 1/4-ounce) cans fruit cocktail, drained
1 cup sugar
3/4 teaspoon pure vanilla extract
1/4 teaspoon ground cinnamon
1/4 teaspoon salt

Preheat the oven to 275 degrees. Grease a 13 x 9-inch pan. Cook the noodles as directed on the package, to al dente. Drain and rinse with cold water. Drain again. Set aside.

In a large bowl, beat eggs. Add the fruit cocktail, sugar, vanilla, cinnamon, and salt. Stir constantly, cooking until the sugar is completely dissolved. Stir in the noodles. Pour into a greased pan. Bake for 1 hour and 15 minutes, or until the egg mixture is set and the top is a light brown.

Serves 12

Ben's Kosher Delicatessen Potato Salad

2 1/2 pounds red potatoes (of uniform size)
1/2 carrot, minced
1/2 green bell pepper, minced
1/2 yellow onion, minced
1 cup mayonnaise
4 tablespoons distilled white vinegar
2 tablespoons sugar
1 teaspoon salt
1/8 teaspoon ground white pepper

Boil the potatoes until they are very tender when pierced with a knife. Drain and rinse with water. Cool slightly. When cool to the touch, peel and discard the skin. Chop the potatoes into 1/2-inch chunks.

In a large bowl, combine the potatoes, carrots, green pepper, and onions. Set aside. In a small bowl, whisk together the mayonnaise, vinegar, sugar, salt, and pepper. Pour over the potato mixture. Toss until the potatoes are thoroughly coated. For a creamier texture, mash a few potatoes while mixing. Refrigerate until it is chilled, approximately 1 hour.

Serves 6 to 8 (6 cups)

Ben's Kosher Delicatessen Coleslaw

    1 large green cabbage, cored, cleaned, and, shredded

    1/3 cup minced carrots

    2 tablespoons minced yellow onions

    2 tablespoons minced green bell pepper

    1 cup mayonnaise

    2 1/2 tablespoons sugar

    1 tablespoon white distilled vinegar

    3/4 teaspoon salt

    Pinch of white pepper

In a large bowl, combine the cabbage, carrots, onions, and green pepper. Set aside. In a small bowl, use a whisk to whip together the mayonnaise, sugar, vinegar, salt, and white pepper. Pour the mayonnaise mixture over the cabbage mixture. Toss until the cabbage is thoroughly coated. Refrigerate until the coleslaw is chilled, approximately 1 hour.

Serves 6 to 8 (6 cups)

Ben's Kosher Delicatessen Tzimmes

    1/2 pound margarine

    4 large carrots, peeled and sliced

    2 medium yams, peeled and sliced

    1 cup freshly squeezed orange juice

    1 cup unsweetened pineapple juice

    1 cup brown sugar

    1 cup granulated sugar

    1 cup honey

    1/2 teaspoon allspice

    2 tablespoons cornstarch

    2 cups pitted prunes

Melt the margarine in a large saucepan. Add the carrots and yams, and sauté until they are fork tender. Add the remaining ingredients except for the prunes, and bring to a boil. Reduce the heat and simmer until the vegetables are soft, about 30 minutes. Add the prunes and cook until it is just heated through. Serve it as a side dish.

Serves 10

Photo, 1975. *(Courtesy of Carnegie Deli)*

"I make a Gooooood Sandwich"

Critics declare Carnegie Deli's pastrami and corned beef "THE TOPS"

Menu art, circa 1955. One of the only surviving menus from Carnegie Deli's earlier days. *(Courtesy of Carnegie Deli)*

Carnegie Deli

From the foot-high sandwiches to the surly wait staff to the countermen in the front yelling out the orders, Carnegie Deli is the quintessential New York deli. The corned beef sandwich here is two inches higher than any of the competition, and the triple-decker combos with pastrami, tongue, and salami are off-the-chart huge!

Carnegie's motto is to keep it simple, make it yourself, do it better than anyone else, and don't be greedy, and it's been done this way since opening in its same location in 1937. When it opened, the Carnegie Deli was poised for greatness. Situated near Carnegie Hall, the deli attracted the elegant attendees of this landmark venue along with members of the broadcast media, whose offices were near Times Square and the Theater District. Under the ownership of Izzie and Ida Orgel, the menu was considerably smaller than it is today. From a small kitchen, it quickly became known for its brisket, flanken, chicken in the pot, matzo ball soup, chopped liver, strudel, and rice pudding. Max Hudes was the next owner, and he ran the deli for thirty-four years before selling it to Leo Steiner and Milton Parker in 1976. It was then that the mystique of the Carnegie began to take shape. Their goal was just to make a decent profit at the end of the day, but so much more than that happened. Within three years, lines for a seat at one of Carnegie's tables began to form all the way outside.

The list of celebrities who have frequented the Carnegie reads like a playbill. There was even a special "comedians" table in the front where the likes of Milton Berle, Joey Adams, Jackie Mason, and Henny Youngman once held court and ate for free.

In 1988 The Pastrami Wars, an event inspired by the local media, pitted the Stage Deli, which is located just steps away on Seventh Avenue, against the Carnegie Deli for the best of the best in cured meats. The competition and the publicity didn't hurt either of them, but in the end, because the Carnegie Deli cured its own meats, albeit in New Jersey with New Jersey water, it came out on top.

Milton Parker passed away in 2009 at ninety years old, but his son-in-law, Sandy Levine, continues the long and worthy tradition of catering to tourists and locals alike. And even with the constant arrival of tour buses, the food here rates at the top, and no tourist with a guidebook would dare miss dining at this corned beef palace.

Carnegie Deli Cheesecake

Cookie crust:

1 cup all-purpose flour

1/4 cup sugar

1 teaspoon grated lemon zest

1/2 teaspoon pure vanilla extract

1 egg yolk

1/2 cup (1 stick) unsalted butter, chilled
   and cut into 1/4-inch pieces

Filling:

1 1/4 pounds cream cheese, at room temperature

3/4 cup sugar

1 1/2 tablespoon all-purpose flour

1 1/2 teaspoon freshly squeezed lemon juice

1 1/2 teaspoon pure vanilla extract

3 eggs, plus 1 egg yolk

2 tablespoons heavy whipping cream

To make the crust, butter and flour the bottom of a 9 x 2-inch springform pan. Place all the ingredients in a large mixing bowl. With your fingertips, rub the ingredients together until they are well mixed and can be gathered into a ball. Dust with a little flour, wrap in waxed paper, and refrigerate for at least 1 hour.

Preheat oven to 350 degrees.

Roll out a piece of dough to cover the bottom of the springform pan. The dough should be as thick as for a sugar cookie (1/4 inch). Reserve the remaining dough. Bake at 350 degrees until it is a light brown. Remove the pan from the oven and cool it on a cooling rack.

Butter the sides of the springform pan. Roll out the remaining dough and line the sides of the pan. Trim the excess dough from the edges. Set aside.

To make the filling, place the cream cheese in a large mixing bowl and beat vigorously with a wooden spoon until creamy and smooth. Beat in the sugar a few tablespoons at a time. When it is well incorporated, beat in the flour, lemon, vanilla, eggs and egg yolk, and heavy cream. There should be no lumps.

Preheat the oven to 485 to 500 degrees. (A hot oven enhances the color of the cheesecake.) Pour the filling into the dough-lined pan and bake in the center of the oven until a golden brown color has been achieved, about 10 minutes. The cake should also start to rise slightly. Remove the cake from the oven and let it cool for 30 minutes.

Set the oven temperature to 350 degrees.

After 30 minutes return the cheesecake to the oven for a final baking to set the cake. Remember that cheesecake is like a pudding, with only eggs used to firm the cake. When the cake is bouncy in the center and slightly raised in the middle as well on the sides, it's finished. Cooking times will vary (usually 25 to 40 minutes) due to variances in ovens. It's very similar to baking a flan or a quiche: overbake, and the cake will crack and be firm; underbake, and the cake will tend to be soft in the center.

Cool for at least 2 hours before attempting to remove the cake from the pan. It is best to refrigerate it overnight, then remove the cake and allow it to come close to room temperature. Always cut slices with a hot, wet knife.

Serves 12

Carnegie Deli
Matzo Ball Soup

This is a good recipe for a crowd. Reducing it would take away its flavor.

 30 eggs
 2 1/3 cups liquid shortening or olive oil
 2 cups water
 5 pounds matzo meal
 Salt and pepper, to taste

In a large bowl, mix the eggs, shortening, water, matzo meal, and salt and pepper. The mixture should be thick but manageable. Place in the refrigerator for about 30 minutes to chill. This makes the mixture easier to handle. Remove from the refrigerator and, by hand, form round balls about the size of a billiard ball. Add the balls to Carnegie Deli Consommè (see below) and boil for 45 minutes.

Serves 20

Carnegie Deli
Chicken Consommé

Like Carnegie Deli Matzo Ball Soup, this is another recipe that best suits a crowd.

 1 (1 pound) chicken, cut up
 1 tablespoon chicken base or bouillon
 1 stalk celery
 1 small white onion
 Salt and pepper, to taste
 1/2 gallon water

Put all of the ingredients in a large pot, cover with the water, bring to a boil, and simmer for 2 hours. Skim the surface with a spoon to remove the fat residue.

Serves 20

Carnegie Deli
Kreplach with Meat

 Dough:
 1 cup all-purpose flour
 1/2 teaspoon salt
 2 eggs
 1 tablespoon warm water

 Filling:
 1/2 pound chopped ground beef (use lean
  meat such as ground round)
 1 small green onion, chopped
 1 egg, beaten
 Salt and pepper, to taste

To make the dough, in a large mixing bowl, mix all of the ingredients with a mixer until the dough is smooth. Roll it out and slice it into 8 pieces. Dust a work surface with flour and roll out each of the 8 pieces to 1/8-inch thickness. Cut out about 4 circles (approximately 3 inches in diameter) from each piece.

To make the filling, sauté the meat and onion at the same time, until the meat is brown and then stir in the egg, salt, and pepper. Place 1/2 teaspoon of the meat mixture into each dough circle. Fold in half and pinch the edges tight to seal. Pull the edges of the half circle back and pinch to form a triangle. Drop the kreplach one at a time into boiling water and cook for 15 minutes. Remove the kreplach with a slotted spoon, and add to soup or serve as a side dish.

Serves 30

EISENBERG'S Sandwich Shop

Photo, 1990. The lunch crowd at the busy and classic Eisenberg's Sandwich Shop.
(Courtesy Eisenberg's Sandwich Shop and Chrystie Sherman)

Eisenberg's Sandwich Shop

Eisenberg's may be called a sandwich shop, but don't let that fool you. Eisenberg's is a deli in the true sense of the word. Established in 1929 by Eli Eisenberg and his brothers, the narrow luncheonette-style coffee shop/deli hasn't changed a bit since it opened that fateful year. The original long, green marble counter spans the length of the room, with just a few small Formica tables lining the walls. Work your way to the back and you're in Phil's "Hawaiian Room," a section of the counter that an old-time waiter — Phil — named as his section of the counter.

But it's not the décor that has brought in the throngs for almost eighty years; it's the best tuna fish sandwich in New York. The usual deli staples like corned beef, pastrami, and chopped liver sandwiches, the special matzo ball soup, and the specialty meat loaf sandwich also contribute to everyone's happiness in this upscale neighborhood. You can get a real egg cream here or a lime rickey made in front of you by countermen, who look like they have been there since Eisenberg's opened and are always ready to kibbitz with the customers. The original coffee urn is still percolating, and the unique wooden boards, which serve as the menus, still hang along the back of the counter. The prices, too, have changed little since the deli's opening so long ago.

Steve Oh, the third owner of Eisenberg's, has no plans for change in this New York City landmark. Why should he? When the counter seats are filled at any given time of day, you know you have something that just works.

Famous 4th Street Deli

When Samuel Auspitz came to America from Hungary at thirteen years old, his entry was far from smooth. Almost upon arrival, he was hit by a truck and spent the next three months in Bellevue Hospital in New York City. Samuel had left a colorful past in the Carpathian Mountains, and the life of New York City was not for him. As soon as his leg healed, he moved on, settling in historic Philadelphia. His father, who was in the horse-hair mattress business in Hungary, sent one child after another to America as his finances permitted until all five of his sons were safe in the new country. It was then that the Auspitz brothers entered the deli business.

In 1923 the Famous 4th Street Deli opened its doors in what was then the predominantly Jewish part of Philadelphia. The building, which is located on the corner of 4th and Bainbridge streets, remains unchanged today, offering a steady link to the past. Movie audiences got a taste of the deli's distinctive charm when it was featured in the 1993 movie *Philadelphia*, with Denzel Washington and Tom Hanks.

It was Samuel Auspitz's wife, Florence, who realized that the days of strictly counter service were numbered when chain stores began to proliferate. She suggested they add a few tables to the deli, making it more of a family-friendly place. The couple kept the deli mentality going strong. If a customer didn't have exact change or was unable to pay, Samuel took care of it. This is the true charm of the business: it's personal. And it's the personality of the business that keeps the customers coming back.

David Auspitz, Samuel's son, eventually took the helm along with his wife, who makes the "Famous" cookies. David has enjoyed a lifetime of good cooking. He knows the secrets, passed along to him by his mother. "The brisket is cooked to death," says David, "the way it's supposed to be. The longer it cooks, the better it gets!" David says he feels a bond with other deli men. He is passionate about his love for deli and deli culture, and he speaks with love about his parents and their dedication to the life they chose. "No other kind of restaurant will have the stories a deli will," says David. "When you make a deal in the deli, it stands."

The menu at Famous 4th Street Deli reads like a deli menu of days gone by. There is the traditional deli fare with only one addition, the chef salad. And appetizers, fish, and the like, are sold alongside deli meats.

It's good when you have loyal customers, loyal employees, good friends, and famous celebrities who come often to your restaurant.

In 2005 the Auspitz's sold the deli to Russ Cowen, a fourth generation deliman from Brooklyn. The deli now cures its own pastrami and has a full-service bakery. The history of the delicatessen continues.

Photo, 1923. This cavernous space was the original location for Famous 4th Street Deli. Like many delis back in the 1920s, it sold pickles, olives, and herring from barrels. *(Courtesy of Famous 4th Street Deli)*

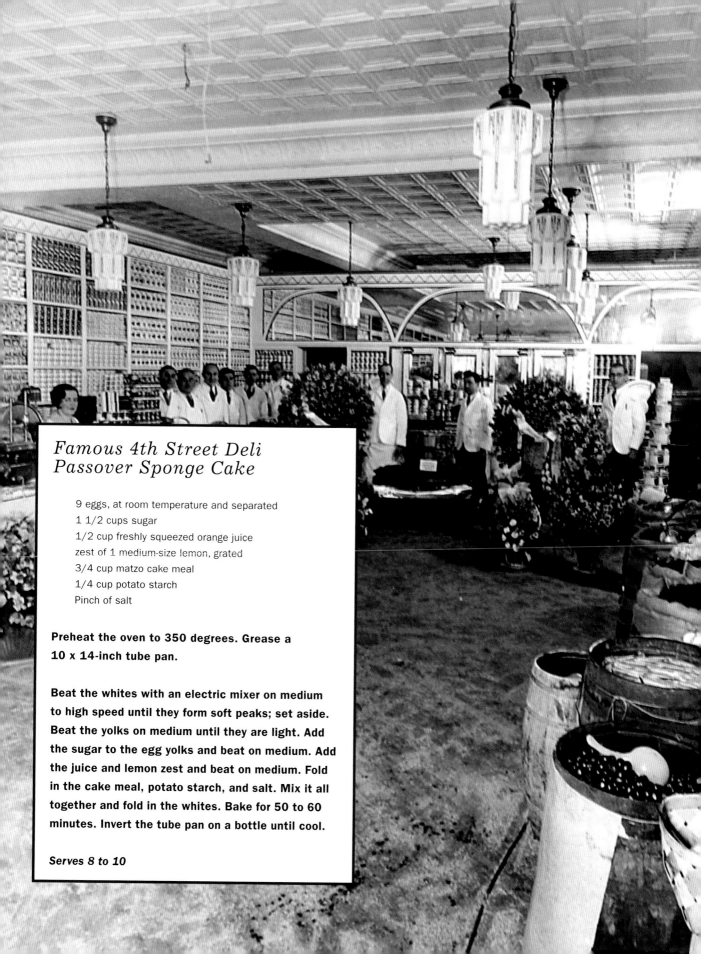

Famous 4th Street Deli Passover Sponge Cake

9 eggs, at room temperature and separated
1 1/2 cups sugar
1/2 cup freshly squeezed orange juice
zest of 1 medium-size lemon, grated
3/4 cup matzo cake meal
1/4 cup potato starch
Pinch of salt

Preheat the oven to 350 degrees. Grease a
10 x 14-inch tube pan.

Beat the whites with an electric mixer on medium
to high speed until they form soft peaks; set aside.
Beat the yolks on medium until they are light. Add
the sugar to the egg yolks and beat on medium. Add
the juice and lemon zest and beat on medium. Fold
in the cake meal, potato starch, and salt. Mix it all
together and fold in the whites. Bake for 50 to 60
minutes. Invert the tube pan on a bottle until cool.

Serves 8 to 10

Photo, circa 1920. Pushcart vendor. *(Courtesy of Rabbi Peter Schweitzer)*

Business card, date unknown. *(Courtesy of Rabbi Peter Schweitzer)*

Famous 4th Street Deli Chopped Liver

1 pound chicken livers
4 tablespoons schmaltz (chicken fat)
2 yellow onions, diced
3 hard-boiled egg yolks
1 teaspoon salt, plus more as needed
1/4 teaspoon freshly ground black pepper,
    plus more as needed

Wash the livers and remove any discolored spots. Drain. Heat 2 tablespoons of the schmaltz in a frying pan. Add the onions and sauté until brown. Remove the onions from the pan and set aside, reserving the fat in the pan. Cook the livers in the remaining fat, stirring occasionally, for 10 minutes. Transfer the onions, livers, and egg yolks to the meat grinder and grind or chop to a smooth texture. Add the salt, pepper, and the remaining chicken fat. Mix it together and taste it for seasoning. Serve the chopped liver cold as a spread with crackers or in spoonfuls on lettuce leaves.

Serves 6 as an appetizer, 12 as a spread

Famous 4th Street Deli Passover Banana Cake

1 cup matzo cake meal
1/4 cup potato starch
1 1/2 cups sugar
1 teaspoon salt
1/2 cup peanut oil
8 eggs, separated
1 cup mashed bananas
2 teaspoons grated lemon zest

Preheat the oven to 325 degrees.

Combine the cake meal, potato starch, sugar, and salt in a mixing bowl. Make a well in the center. Add the oil, egg yolks, bananas, and lemon zest. Beat the mixture on medium until it is very smooth, about 5 minutes with an electric mixer. In a separate bowl, beat the egg whites until they are very stiff. Do not underbeat. Pour the egg yolk mixture slowly over the whites; gently fold in until it is just blended. Do not stir. Pour into an ungreased 10-inch tube pan and bake for 1 hour and 10 minutes, or until golden. Invert the pan immediately onto a bottle to cool.

Serves 4 to 6

Gertel's
BAKE SHOPPE

Gertel's Bake Shoppe

Before moving locations in 2007, this kosher bakery extraordinaire had been located at 53 Hester Street, right in the heart of the Lower East Side in New York City, since opening its doors in 1914. Although this bastion of kosher baked goods and pastries has moved its wholesale and retail business to the Williamsburg section of Brooklyn, New York, the babkas are still just as delicious. Some ninety years later it is still catering to locals, tourists, and delis across the country.

Gertel's has an amazing display of some 300 items, but its specialties are the gorgeous challahs, babkas, and rugelach. Gertel's may very well make the best raspberry, apricot, chocolate, and cinnamon raisin rugelach in the city. It's also one of the few places that makes teiglach, an Old World pastry that is rarely found anymore. Teiglach is a sweet roll made of pastry nuggets held together by honey and covered with nuts and candied cherries.

You can nibble on this pastry for weeks (at least in theory!) as the honey acts as a preservative.

Israel Moskowitz, the diet-conscious, thin-as-a-rail master baker at Gertel's, begins his day at 2:00 a.m., baking some 1,000 babkas daily, in addition to all the other delicious pastries.

The faded sign over the bakery reads "baking done on premises." If you get there when the buttery rugelach are brought out from the cavernous kitchen, count your blessings!

Product label, 2004. *(Courtesy of Gertel's Bake Shoppe)*

Gertel's Bake Shoppe
Chocolate Babkas

1/2 cup active yeast

4 1/4 cups warm water

1 3/4 cups sugar

2 eggs, plus 2 egg yolks, beaten

1 1/4 pounds (5 sticks) margarine

1 1/2 teaspoons salt

10 cups all-purpose flour

1 1/2 teaspoons pure vanilla extract

Chocolate filling:

1/2 cup cocoa

2 cups sugar

1/4 teaspoon vanilla

Pinch of salt

Preheat the oven to 300 degrees.

In a large bowl dissolve the yeast in 1/4 cup of warm water, stir in the sugar, and let stand for 10 minutes until foamy. Add the remaining water, eggs, margarine, salt, flour, and vanilla and use an electric mixer to mix until the dough holds together and achieves a shine. The dough should be soft and slightly warm. Turn out the dough on a lightly oiled board, knead, cover, and allow it to rise for 30 minutes.

Meanwhile, make the filling. Mix together the cocoa, sugar, vanilla, and pinch of salt. Lightly grease eight 9 x 5 1/2-inch loaf pans.

Divide the dough into 4 parts. Oil your hands and stretch the dough by pulling portions with your hands to equal the length of the pan. Sprinkle 1/4 of the chocolate filling onto each section of the dough. Begin to twist and turn the dough starting at the bottom so the chocolate mixture runs throughout. Cut each piece in half, place the halves in a loaf pans and allow them to rise for 30 minutes. Bake the halves at 300 degrees for 30 minutes. Cool, slice, and serve.

Serves 55 (8 loaf-sized babkas)

Junior's

When times were good and when times were bad, Brooklyn's Junior's deli was there for you. This is where comfort food got its meaning, where people came for a sense of kinship. Junior's is in a class of its own, and no book on delis would be complete without it. It is both a restaurant and a full-service deli, and, as they say, "If we have it, we'll make it, you'll get it."

Menu, 2002. *(Courtesy of Junior's)*

One cannot speak of Junior's without first speaking about Brooklyn and the rich cultural environment that existed there in the early part of the twentieth century. The corner of DeKalb and Flatbush Avenue was the site of the Enduro Sandwich Shop that Harry and Mike Rosen opened in 1929, oddly named for a stainless steel equipment company that Harry liked. The last in a series of three sandwich shops that the brothers opened, the Enduro existed in the shadow of the enormous Brooklyn Paramount Theater sign, in a neighborhood flourishing with theaters such as the Albee and the palatial Fox, where stars like Jack Benny, Mae West, and Burns and Allen performed. This was a neighborhood thriving with culture. Then the stock market crashed and the Rosen brothers sold the other sandwich shops to concentrate on the Enduro. Times were grim and the Depression and Prohibition cast a dark shadow over America. By the time Prohibition was repealed, Harry Rosen realized his dream of a full-scale restaurant and bar in the heart of downtown Brooklyn.

Brooklyn is a who's who of the entertainment world. Imagine a place where Mickey Rooney grew up, where Eddie Canter worked as a waiter, where the Gershwin brothers composed music and Henry Miller was born, where Mel Brooks, Jackie Mason, Jack Gilford, Jackie Gleason, Dom DeLuise, Mary Tyler Moore, Joan Rivers, Jimmy Durante, Jerry Stiller, and Phil Silvers learned what funny was. Brooklyn is where Eli Wallach, Paul Sorvino, and Elliot Gould learned to act and Beverly Sills, Barbra Streisand, Lena Horne, Steve Lawrence, and Edie Gorme began their singing careers. Great writers including Joseph Heller and Isaac Bashevis Singer and scientist Carl Sagan also lived in Brooklyn. Woody Allen resided here, Pete Hamill learned the tricks of journalism here, and playwrights such as Adolph Green and Betty Comden honed their skills on this side of the Brooklyn Bridge. And the list goes on. One can only imagine that every one of these "locals" met at the Enduro and then Junior's for a cup of steaming matzo ball soup or a plate of cheese blintzes after the theater or a ball game. This place, this Brooklyn, was the center for culture, religion, education, ethnic diversity, and, yes — great food!

But World War II changed everything. After the war, people began moving to the suburbs, and in 1949 the Enduro closed. People from the community, friends and strangers alike, pulled together to help rebuild and refurbish the old Enduro, and finally

did so in 1950. Harry Rosen changed the name of the restaurant to Junior's in honor of his two sons, Marvin and Walter. And today Walter's two sons, Kevin and Alan, are at the helm of this famous deli. Overstuffed brisket sandwiches, creamy potato salad, and smooth egg creams are back, and so are the many happy customers!

Junior's may have a few forbidden, non-kosher foods, but in this new world of changing neighborhoods and demographics, delis need to adapt to the times. The menu here keeps getting bigger; items are added and never taken away. And if you

Junior's Reuben Sandwiches

Making any of these sandwiches requires some skill and timing, as the parts come together quickly on a hot skillet or grill. Read through the instructions before you start to avoid burning the sandwich.

Classic Reuben:

6 ounces corned beef, sliced

4 ounces sauerkraut

4 slices Swiss cheese

2 slices rye bread

Russian (Thousand Island) dressing

Turkey Reuben:

6 ounces turkey, sliced

4 ounces sauerkraut

4 slices Swiss cheese

2 slices rye bread

Russian (Thousand Island) dressing

Pastrami Reuben:

6 ounces Romanian pastrami, sliced

4 ounces sauerkraut

4 slices Swiss cheese

2 slices rye bread

Russian (Thousand Island) dressing

Combo Reuben:

6 ounces corned beef, sliced

6 ounces pastrami, sliced

4 ounces sauerkraut

4 slices Swiss cheese

2 slices rye bread

Russian (Thousand Island) dressing

Butter both sides of the rye bread slices and place them in a skillet over medium-low heat. As they grill, warm the meat and sauerkraut in a separate skillet until both are heated all the way through. Flip the bread slices and top 1 bread slice with 2 slices of cheese followed by the meat, sauerkraut, remaining 2 slices of cheese, and remaining bread slice. Continue warming until the cheese melts, flipping once. Serve with Russian dressing on the side if you wish.

Serves 1 (each makes 1 large sandwich)

are a regular you already know that anything that doesn't appear on the menu can be yours for the asking, whether it's Belgian waffles, creamy mashed potatoes, or a mountain-high vanilla sundae.

The criterion for true deli dining requires a table loaded with pickles, bowls of Romanian coleslaw, beets, pickled onions, and peppers. And then, of course, there's the bread. Junior's wins the prize for the best breadbasket in America. Heaped high with freshly baked goods, it delivers cinnamon rolls, rugelach, and blueberry muffins for breakfast, and cornbread and onion and Vienna rolls hot out of the oven for lunch and dinner. And the basket is bottomless, filled before you even notice.

Walking into Junior's, you are welcomed with one of the most scrumptious baked goods counter ever. And, of course, not to be missed are Junior's specialty cheesecakes with their thinly baked sponge crust; this is heaven on a plate!

So many delis have closed in other cities that one might worry, but Junior's isn't going anywhere. Instead, in 2006 Junior's opened a second branch of the deli on 45th Street in the heart of the theater district in New York City. The bottomless bread

basket doesn't happen at this second location, but the tradition of a great deli still exists.

Junior's Famous No. 1 Cheesecake

Sponge cake layer:

1/2 cup cake flour, sifted

1 teaspoon baking powder

Pinch of salt

3 extra-large eggs, separated

1/3 cup plus 2 tablespoons granulated sugar

1 teaspoon pure vanilla extract

3 drops pure lemon extract

3 tablespoons unsalted butter, melted

1/4 teaspoon cream of tartar

Cream cheese filling:

4 (8-ounce) packages cream cheese, at room temperature

1 2/3 cups sugar

1/4 cup cornstarch

1 tablespoon pure vanilla extract

2 extra-large eggs

3/4 cup heavy whipping cream

To make the sponge cake layer, preheat the oven to 350 degrees. Generously butter a 9-inch springform pan.

Sift the cake flour, baking powder, and salt together in a bowl and set aside. Beat egg yolks in a large bowl with an electric mixer on high speed for 3 minutes. With the mixer running, gradually add 1/3 cup of the sugar and continue beating until thick, light yellow ribbons form in the bowl, about 5 minutes more. Beat in the vanilla and lemon extracts. Sift the flour mixture over the batter and stir it in by hand until no more white flecks appear. Blend in the butter.

In a clean bowl, using clean, dry beaters, beat the egg whites and cream of tartar together on high speed until frothy. Gradually add the remaining 2 tablespoons of sugar and continue beating until stiff peaks form. (The whites should stand up in stiff peaks but not be dry.) Stir about 1/3 cup of the whites into the batter, then gently fold in the remaining whites — don't worry if a few white specks remain. Gently spoon the batter into the pan. Bake the cake just until the center of the cake springs back when lightly touched, only about 10 minutes (watch carefully). Let the cake cool in the pan on a wire rack while you make the cheesecake filling. Do not remove the cake from the pan.

While cake cools, make the cream cheese filling. Place 1 package of the cream cheese, 1/3 cup of the sugar, and the cornstarch in a large bowl. Beat with an electric mixer on low speed until creamy, about 3 minutes. Then beat in the remaining 3 packages of cream cheese. Increase the mixer speed to high and beat in the remaining 1 1/3 cups of the sugar, and then beat in the

vanilla. Blend in the eggs, one at a time, beating the batter well after adding each addition. Blend in the heavy cream. Mix the filling just until completely blended. Do not overmix. Gently spoon the cheese filling on top of the cooled sponge cake layer. Place the springform pan in a large shallow pan containing hot water that comes about 1-inch up the sides of the pan. Bake the cheesecake until the center barely jiggles when you shake the pan, about 1 hour.

Remove the cake from the oven and cool in the pan on a wire rack for 1 hour. Then cover the cake with plastic wrap and refrigerate until completely cold, at least 4 hours or overnight. Remove the sides of the springform pan. Slide the cake off the bottom of the pan onto a serving plate. Or, if you wish, simply leave the cake on the removable bottom of the pan and place it on a serving plate. If any cake is left over, cover it with plastic wrap and store it in the refrigerator for up to one week.

Serves 12

Katz's Deli

Upon entering Katz's Deli you are met with the same intoxicating smell of pickling spices, grilled hot dogs, and steamed corned beef and pastrami that people have been experiencing for over a century. Katz's has the distinction of being the oldest kosher-style deli in New York City. In the city that started it all, Katz's is still thriving.

Katz's Deli began across the street from its present location in 1888, but due to the need to construct the New York subway system, the deli moved to the corner of Ludlow and Houston in the early 1900s. Katz's became a focal point for the newly emigrated families from Eastern Europe to gather, share stories, compare notes, and do what they loved to do best — eat!

Hardly changed since the beginning of the twentieth century, except for the Formica tables and fluorescent lighting, at Katz's you can sit down to enjoy a hot, spicy pastrami sandwich, close your eyes, and reckon back to times that were difficult, sometimes lonely, but also hopeful for a future that held promise. Katz's reputation for a loyal following has remained constant for generations of immigrants, residents, and visitors to New York.

It all started with Willy Katz, who partnered with the Iceland brothers to open a deli. Some years later, he and his brother bought the deli from them. And when the sign painter hired to paint the sign in front of the building asked Mr. Katz what he would like it to read, he answered, "Katz's, that's all." It has remained that way ever since.

Everyone eats here, including celebrities, politicians, and four United States presidents as well as locals and a huge tourist crowd. You could spend hours eating and gazing at the hundreds of photographs lining the walls of this vintage deli, which still bears the tin ceiling that has been here since its opening.

Three hundred customers can fill the tables in Katz's Deli, and that is what you will find every day and late into the night. You can opt to have a waiter serve you, or order for yourself from the counterman. It goes like this: you enter (it's loud and raucous); you're given a entry ticket which serves as your tab; you search for a table and lay your coat on a chair when you find it; you go to the counter; you are offered "tastes" of the pastrami or corned beef; and then you make a decision. The choices are endless and the smells could leave you weak in the knees. The light-as-a-feather matzo ball soup, hot pastrami on rye bread, or two grilled Katz's hot dogs with sauerkraut are among the many choices. By this time, you hope the throngs of people lined up behind you haven't started yelling at you yet. Then you grab a drink, find your table again (it could be inhabited by a group of tourists looking for the table made famous in the movie *When Harry Met Sally*), and start to eat. This might be the best pastrami sandwich you will ever eat. And don't forget to present your ticket before you exit.

Katz's corned beef is made on the premises, and Katz's salamis are famous. The three-meat platter "feeds two tourists or one regular customer." And asking for mayonnaise is a no-no! (It isn't kosher.)

During World War II, the three Katz sons served in the armed forces. A sign hanging over the deli counter still says it all: "Send a Salami to Your Boy in the Army." But you don't have to do that. You can eat one all by yourself.

Opposite page: (Top left) Photo, 2004; (Top right) Photo, 2004; (Bottom) Photo, 1932; the classic cast of characters in the front of Katz's in the early 1930s. (Courtesy of Katz's Deli and Yura Dashevsky)

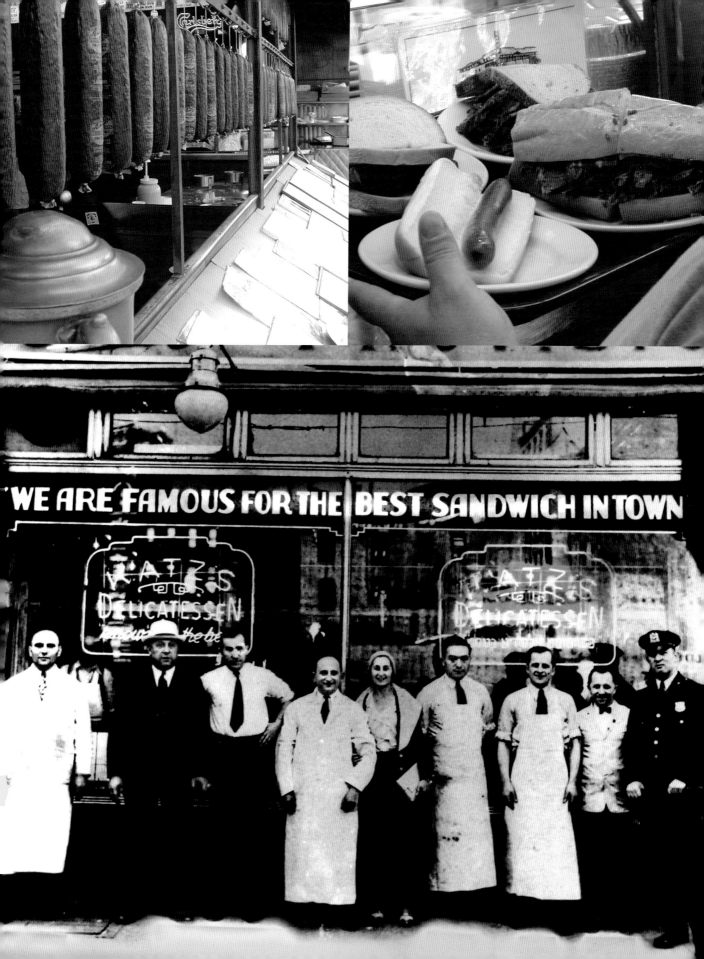

Katz's Deli Honey Cake

3 1/2 cups all-purpose flour, sifted

2 1/2 teaspoons baking powder

1 teaspoon baking soda

1 teaspoon ground cinnamon

1/2 teaspoon ground cloves

1 cup sugar

3 eggs, separated

1/4 cup vegetable oil

1 1/3 cups honey

1 1/3 cups warm black coffee

1 teaspoon cream of tartar

1 cup chopped walnuts (optional)

Preheat the oven to 350 degrees. Lightly grease a 9-inch tube pan.

Mix and sift the flour, baking powder, baking soda, cinnamon, cloves, and sugar into a large bowl. Make a well and add the egg yolks, oil, honey, and coffee. Beat the mixture until it is smooth. Beat the egg whites with the cream of tartar until very stiff peaks stand. Fold into the batter (do not beat or stir). Add the walnuts. Pour into the prepared tube pan. Bake for 55 to 60 minutes, or until golden.

Serves 6 to 8

Katz's Deli Lokshen Kugel

16 ounces wide egg noodles

1/2 teaspoon salt

6 eggs

1/2 cup (1 stick) butter

1 cup milk

1 cup sour cream

1 (12-ounce) can unsweetened pineapple slices

1 (12-ounce) can Mandarin orange slices

1/2 cup golden raisins

1/2 teaspoon ground cinnamon

1 teaspoon pure vanilla extract

Preheat the oven to 350 degrees. Grease a 9 x 12 pan.

Cook the noodles in salted boiling water according to the package directions. Drain and cool in an ice water bath. Whisk the eggs in a bowl with melted butter, milk, and sour cream. Toss with the noodles and add the remaining ingredients. Place in the prepared pan, cover tightly with aluminum foil, and bake for 1/2 hour. Remove the cover and cook for 10 minutes more to allow it to brown. Slice and serve.

Serves 10 to 12

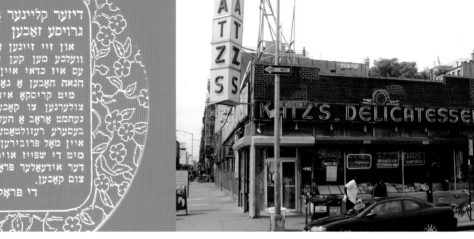

Katz's Deli Borscht

1 quart water

4 fresh beets, grated

1 cup chopped yellow onion

Salt, to taste

2 teaspoons sugar

freshly squeezed lemon juice

Sour cream, for serving

Combine the water, beets, onion, and salt in a large stockpot and bring them to a boil. Cook for 1/2 hour on low heat. Stir in the sugar and lemon juice. Cook 10 minutes more. Refrigerate the mixture to chill, about 30 minutes. Serve the borscht topped with a dollop of sour cream.

Serves 4

Katz's Deli Shav Soup (Sorrel)

1 pound sorrel (sour grass)

1/2 pound spinach

2 quarts water

Salt and pepper, to taste

Freshly squeezed lemon juice, to taste

Sugar, to taste

2 tablespoons sour cream

Sliced scallions, for garnish

Wash the greens and tear or chop into pieces. Combine the greens in a pot with spinach and water and bring to a boil. Reduce the heat and simmer for 30 minutes, stirring frequently. Add the salt, pepper, lemon juice, and sugar. Cook 15 minutes more, then remove from the heat and let it cool.

To serve, add 1 tablespoon of sour cream and 1 tablespoon of soup to a soup bowl, and stir them to combine. Fill the bowl with soup, top with the scallions, and serve hot.

Serves 6 to 8

Postcard, 1946. Lindy's prime location on the corner
of Broadway and 50th Street near Times Square.
(Courtesy of Jeffrey Segal)

Lindy's

As long as there is Broadway and the Broadway theaters, there will always be nostalgia for Lindy's, a deli that in its heyday was the most well-known of all the delis in the Theater District in New York City.

In 1921, eight years after immigrating to America, Leo and Clara Lindermann opened Lindy's. A second deli soon followed, but the one that remains today is on Seventh Avenue and 53rd Street, just minutes from Times Square. This was the original Broadway Deli, the place where actors and vaudevillians would congregate before and after the shows. Lindy's became a hangout for some of the biggest stars of the day, like Eddie Canter, Al Jolson, and the Marx Brothers. To say that the clientele was colorful was an understatement. It was a place for politicians to campaign, a place for celebrities to mingle with each other, and a haven for gangsters to congregate. It was here that Walter Winchell wrote and then phoned-in his column from his own private booth. Writer Damon Runyon was a regular at Lindy's. He immortalized Lindy's (calling it "Mindy's") in his musical, *Guys and Dolls*. In this 1950 Broadway production, a bet is wagered between gangsters Sky Masterson and

Nathan Detroit on which was the better seller the previous day, Mindy's cheesecake or its strudel.

But the cheesecake is the thing here. Lindy's created the definitive New York-style cheesecake, the one that sets the standard by which all other cheesecakes are measured. New Yorkers revere Lindy's cheesecake so much that debates and arguments rage from coast to coast, comparing the merits of which deli has the creamiest or the densest cheesecake. Lindy's was the first deli to top its cheesecakes with strawberry or blueberry sauce or all sorts of fresh fruits.

Although Lindy's is one of the few old-time delis remaining that is not family owned, (the Riese Corporation now owns it), the quality of the food and the cheesecake has remained the same as always: a memorable experience from the past.

Lindy's Apple Pancakes with Cinnamon Butter

Cinnamon butter:

1/4 cup (1 stick) unsalted butter,
   at room temperature

1/2 cup confectioners' sugar

1 teaspoon ground cinnamon

1/2 teaspoon grated orange zest

Pancakes:

1 teaspoon freshly squeezed lemon juice

1 teaspoon grated lemon zest

2 Granny Smith apples, peeled, halved, and cored

1 2/3 cups all-purpose flour

2 tablespoons packed light brown sugar

2 1/2 teaspoons baking powder

1/2 teaspoon salt

3/4 cup whole milk

2 large eggs

1/4 cup (1 stick) unsalted butter, melted

To make the cinnamon butter, using an electric mixer on medium speed, beat all the ingredients in a small bowl until they're blended.

To make the pancakes, combine the lemon juice and zest in a bowl. Coarsely grate the apples into a bowl, tossing them to coat them with the juice (this prevents browning). In a separate large bowl, whisk the flour, brown sugar, baking powder, and salt. Make a well in the center of the dry ingredients. Whisk in the milk, eggs, and melted butter until it is smooth. Stir in the apple mixture. Cover and let the batter stand at room temperature for 30 to 60 minutes.

Preheat the oven to 250 degrees. Place a baking sheet in the oven. Heat a heavy, large nonstick griddle or frying pan over medium-high heat for 1 minute. Brush the griddle with some butter. For each pancake, drop 1 heaping tablespoon of batter onto the griddle, spacing pancakes apart. Cook until they are golden on the bottom and bubbles start to form on the surface, about 3 minutes. Turn the pancakes over. Cook until they are golden brown on the bottom, about 2 minutes longer. Transfer the pancakes to a baking sheet in the oven to keep them warm. Repeat with the remaining batter, brushing the griddle with butter before each batch. Arrange on a platter and top with cinnamon butter.

Serves 4

Lindy's Pineapple Glaze

2 tablespoons sugar

4 teaspoons cornstarch

2 (8 1/4-ounce) cans crushed pineapple
in heavy syrup

2 tablespoons freshly squeezed lemon juice

2 drops yellow food coloring

In a small saucepan, combine the sugar and cornstarch. Stir in the remaining ingredients. Over medium heat, bring the mixture to a boil, stirring constantly. Boil for 1 minute, or until it is thickened and translucent. Remove the sauce from the heat and let it cool.

Makes 2 cups

Lindy's Cheesecake

This cheesecake comes with an optional pineapple glaze. With or without, it's divine!

Crumb crust:

1 1/2 cups finely ground graham crackers
or cookies (such as chocolate or vanilla
wafers or gingersnaps)

5 tablespoons unsalted butter, melted

1/3 cup sugar

1/8 teaspoon salt

Filling:

5 (8-ounce) packages cream cheese,
at room temperature

1 3/4 cups sugar

3 tablespoons all-purpose flour

zest of 1 orange, finely grated

zest of 1 lemon, finely grated

5 large eggs, plus 2 large egg yolks

1/2 teaspoon pure vanilla extract

sliced strawberries, for garnish (optional)

To make the crust, stir together all the ingredients and press them into the bottom of a buttered 9-inch springform pan and up the sides about 1 inch. Use it right away or refrigerate for up to 2 hours.

To make the cheesecake, preheat the oven to 550 degrees.

Beat together the cream cheese, sugar, flour, and zests with an electric mixer on medium speed until it's smooth. Add the eggs and yolks, one at a time, and then add the vanilla, beating on low speed until each ingredient is incorporated. Scrape down the bowl between additions.

Put the springform pan with the crust in a shallow baking pan (to catch drips). Pour the filling into the crust (springform pan will be completely full) and bake it in the middle of the oven for 12 minutes, or until puffed. Reduce temperature to 200 degrees and continue baking until the cake is mostly firm, about 1 hour more. The center will be slightly wobbly when the pan is gently shaken.

Run a knife around the top edge of the cake to loosen it, but do not remove it from pan. Cool the cake completely in a pan on a cooling rack. Refrigerate, loosely covered, for at least 6 hours. If using Lindy's Pineapple Glaze (see above), add it now and return the cake to the refrigerator to chill for at least another 3 hours.

Remove the side of the pan and transfer the cake to a plate. Bring it to room temperature before serving it. Cut the cake into wedges using a hot wet knife. Garnish the wedges with strawberries.

Serves 12

Menu art, circa 1960. The cover illustration on a Ratner's bakery menu. *(Courtesy of the Harmatz family)*

Ratner's

There is an old saying that goes, "If you're born in New York, you're born Jewish even if you were baptized."

The old tattered menu at Ratner's reads like a history of the neighborhood it represented, the Lower East Side of New York. Sadly, over time, the neighborhood changed, and the Jewish population that existed there when the restaurant opened in 1905 is no longer.

When Ratner's first opened, half a million Jews lived on the Lower East Side. Throngs of hungry patrons gathered for Ratner's vegetarian and dairy menu (which included the creamiest blintzes), the crispiest latkes, and the most luscious onion rolls in the city, if not the world. No politician would have missed an opportunity to visit Ratner's and mingle with the patrons, shake hands, and campaign for election. Families would gather there for celebrations, bar and bat mitzvahs were held there, and political events often took place there as well. Although the restaurant was dark, dingy, and a little bit cold, no one came for the atmosphere. The somewhat surly waiters didn't seem to bother anyone either. When you were presented with

the heavenly veggie chopped liver, rich kreplach soup, and the warm basket of onion rolls, all was forgiven.

Ratner's famous history is as rich as some of the foods they serve. Gangsters Bugsy Siegel and Meyer Lansky frequented the well-known speakeasy that was hidden in the back of the restaurant during Prohibition; patrons entered through a separate entrance in the back alley. Pictures of the celebrities who dined at Ratner's in later days graced the walls — the likes of Bobby Kennedy, Senator Jacob Javits, Al Capone, as well as countless presidents. In the 1990s, the owners opened the back lounge as a hip "speakeasy-style" nightclub and renamed it Lansky's Lounge, after its famous patron, the notorious gangster Meyer Lansky.

Ratner's ceased being a kosher deli and dropped the kosher certification by Passover 2000. By 2005 there were plans to tear down the famed eatery. New York has lost one of its great institutions, but the memory of Sunday morning brunches and other delicacies at Ratner's will live on for years to come.

Menu art, 1960s–1970s.
(Courtesy of the Harmatz family)

Ratner's Onion Rolls

Dough:

1 package active dry yeast

1 cup lukewarm water

2 tablespoons sugar

1 1/2 teaspoons salt

3/4 cup (about 3) whole eggs

6 tablespoons vegetable oil

4 to 5 cups all-purpose flour

1 egg, well beaten, plus one teaspoon of water

Filling:

2 finely chopped yellow onions (1 cup)

1 teaspoon salt

1 tablespoon poppy seeds

1 1/2 teaspoons caraway seeds

1 cup dry bread crumbs

1/4 cup vegetable oil

In a bowl, soften the yeast by pouring it into a small bowl with one cup of lukewarm water; mix to dissolve. Stir in the sugar, salt, eggs, oil, and enough flour to form stiff dough. Turn the dough out onto a floured work surface and knead it until it is smooth and elastic, about 5 minutes. Place the dough in a greased bowl and turn it to grease the top.

Let it rise, covered, in a warm, dry place until doubled in bulk, about 1 hour. Punch it down and knead it on a floured surface. Roll the dough into an 18 x 24-inch oblong pan. Cut it into twelve 6 x 3-inch pieces.

To prepare the filling, mix all the ingredients in a bowl. Spoon 3/4 of the mixture over the dough pieces. Fold 1/3 of the dough over onions and fold 1/3 over again from the other side. Place the rolls, seam side down, on a greased baking sheet. Flatten until the rolls are 5 inches long. Cut the rolls in half. Brush them with the egg wash and sprinkle them with the remaining mixture. (The rolls can be frozen at this point if you wish. When they are ready to bake, place the frozen rolls on a greased baking sheet and let them rise, uncovered, in a warm place until they have doubled in bulk, about 1 hour. Then bake as directed.) Let them rise, covered, in a warm place until they have doubled in bulk, about 30 minutes.

Preheat the oven to 400 degrees.

Bake the rolls on a baking sheet for 15 to 20 minutes, or until they are golden brown. Cool and serve.

Serves 12 (24 rolls)

Ratner's Vegetable Cutlets

6 (2 pounds) potatoes, peeled and cut into
  2-inch cubes
1/4 cup butter
2 yellow onions, chopped
6 button mushrooms, chopped
1 (14 1/2-ounce) can diced carrots, drained
1 (14 1/2-ounce) can peas, drained
3 eggs
2 cups matzo meal
Salt and freshly ground pepper, to taste

**Preheat the oven to 350 degrees. Grease a
baking sheet.**

**Cook the potatoes in boiling, salted water for
20 minutes, or until they are tender, then mash.
Meanwhile, in a skillet, heat the butter and
sauté the onions and mushrooms until they are
tender. Pour the mushroom mixture into a bowl
with the mashed potatoes. Stir in the carrots,
green beans, peas, and 2 of the eggs. Blend
thoroughly. Add enough matzo meal so that
the mixture can be shaped into large patties.
Season with salt and pepper. Shape into 12 to
15 patties. Beat the remaining egg well. Brush
the patties on both sides with the egg, coating
thoroughly. Place on the baking sheet. Bake
for 45 minutes, or until they are a light golden
brown. Serve with Ratner's Vegetable Cutlet
Gravy (see right).**

Serves 10 to 12 (12 to 15 cutlets)

Ratner's Vegetable Cutlet Gravy

2 pounds button mushrooms, chopped
1 quart water
4 tablespoons butter
1 yellow onion, chopped
1 carrot, diced
1 cup chopped celery
1 green bell pepper, chopped
1 clove garlic, chopped
1 (16-ounce) can whole tomatoes (do not drain)
1 tablespoon mushroom powder or packaged
  dried black mushrooms
1/4 cup all-purpose flour
Salt and pepper, to taste
Paprika, to taste

**In a large saucepan, combine the mushrooms and
water. Simmer for 10 to 15 minutes, until the
mushrooms are tender. Strain the broth.**

**In a saucepan, heat 2 tablespoons of the butter
and sauté the onions, carrots, celery, green
pepper, and garlic until they are soft, about 5
minutes. Add the tomatoes, 3 cups of the mushroom water, and the mushroom powder. (The
remaining 1 cup chopped mushrooms may be
refrigerated in another dish until they are ready to
use.) Simmer on low heat for 20 minutes. Mix the
remaining butter, flour, and enough water to make
a paste. Stir into the saucepan and cook until the
sauce bubbles and thickens, about 10 minutes.
Season with salt, pepper, and paprika. Serve hot,
spooned over Ratner's Vegetable Cutlets (see left).**

Makes 3 cups

Photo, 2003. A bountiful deli display case. *(Courtesy of Russ and Daughters Appetizing Store and Allison Firor)*

Below: Menu, circa 1960. *(Courtesy of the Harmatz family)*

Ratner's Veggie Chopped Liver

- 1/2 pound lentils
- 2 (2 cups) yellow onions, chopped
- 8 hard-boiled eggs
- 3 tablespoons vegetable oil
- 1 tablespoon peanut butter
- 1/4 teaspoon white pepper
- 1 teaspoon salt
- Lettuce leaves, for serving
- Prepared white or red horseradish, for serving
- Sliced tomato, for serving

Cook the lentils according to the package directions. Drain. Put 1/2 cup of the onions into a bowl. In a separate bowl, finely chop the eggs with the lentils and add to the onions. Sauté the remaining onions in 1 1/2 tablespoons of the oil until they are brown. Add the lentil mixture to the sautéed onions. Add the remaining oil, the peanut butter, pepper, and salt. Serve on lettuce leaves with white or red horseradish and a slice of tomato.

Serves 4 to 6

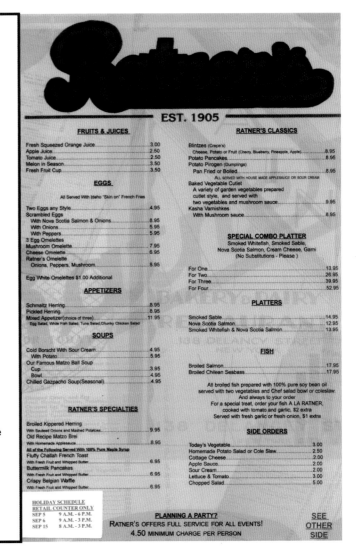

EST. 1905

FRUITS & JUICES

Fresh Squeezed Orange Juice	3.00
Apple Juice	2.50
Tomato Juice	2.50
Melon in Season	3.50
Fresh Fruit Cup	3.50

EGGS

All Served With Idaho "Skin on" French Fries

Two Eggs any Style	4.95
Scrambled Eggs	
With Nova Scotia Salmon & Onions	8.95
With Onions	5.95
With Peppers	5.95
3 Egg Omelettes	
Mushroom Omelette	7.95
Cheese Omelette	6.95
Ratner's Omelette	
Onions, Peppers, Mushroom	8.95
Egg White Omelettes $1.00 Additional	

APPETIZERS

Schmaltz Herring	8.95
Pickled Herring	8.95
Mixed Appetizer(choice of three)	11.95
Egg Salad, White Fish Salad, Tuna Salad,Chunky Chicken Salad	

SOUPS

Cold Borscht With Sour Cream	4.95
With Potato	5.95
Our Famous Matzo Ball Soup	
Cup	3.95
Bowl	4.95
Chilled Gazpacho Soup(Seasonal)	4.95

RATNER'S SPECIALTIES

Broiled Kippered Herring	
With Sauteed Onions and Mashed Potatoes	9.95
Old Recipe Matzo Brei	
With Homemade Applesauce	8.95
All of the Following Served With 100% Pure Maple Syrup	
Fluffy Challah French Toast	
With Fresh Fruit and Whipped Butter	6.95
Buttermilk Pancakes	
With Fresh Fruit and Whipped Butter	6.95
Crispy Belgian Waffle	
With Fresh Fruit and Whipped Butter	6.95

RATNER'S CLASSICS

Blintzes (Crepe's)	
Cheese, Potato or Fruit (Cherry, Blueberry, Pineapple, Apple)	8.95
Potato Pancakes	8.95
Potato Pirogen (Dumplings)	
Pan Fried or Boiled	8.95
ALL SERVED WITH HOUSE MADE APPLESAUCE OR SOUR CREAM	
Baked Vegetable Cutlet	
A variety of garden vegetables prepared	
cutlet style, and served with	
two vegetables and mushroom sauce	9.95
Kasha Varnishkes	
With Mushroom sauce	8.95

SPECIAL COMBO PLATTER

Smoked Whitefish, Smoked Sable,
Nova Scotia Salmon, Cream Cheese, Garni
(No Substitutions - Please)

For One	13.95
For Two	26.95
For Three	39.95
For Four	52.95

PLATTERS

Smoked Sable	14.95
Nova Scotia Salmon	12.95
Smoked Whitefish & Nova Scotia Salmon	13.95

FISH

Broiled Salmon	17.95
Broiled Chilean Seabass	17.95

All broiled fish prepared with 100% pure soy bean oil
served with two vegetables and Chef salad bowl or coleslaw.
And always to your order
For a special treat, order your fish A LA RATNER,
cooked with tomato and garlic, $2 extra
Served with fresh garlic or fresh onion, $1 extra

SIDE ORDERS

Today's Vegetable	3.00
Homemade Potato Salad or Cole Slaw	2.50
Cottage Cheese	2.00
Apple Sauce	2.00
Sour Cream	2.00
Lettuce & Tomato	3.00
Chopped Salad	5.00

**HOLIDAY SCHEDULE
RETAIL COUNTER ONLY**

SEP 5	9 A.M. - 6 P.M.
SEP 6	9 A.M. - 3 P.M.
SEP 15	8 A.M. - 3 P.M.

PLANNING A PARTY?
RATNER'S OFFERS FULL SERVICE FOR ALL EVENTS!
4.50 MINIMUM CHARGE PER PERSON

SEE OTHER SIDE

Ratner's Knishes
(Vegetable and Potato)

Vegetable filling:

1/4 cup vegetable oil

2 1/2 (2 1/2 cups) yellow onions, chopped

1 clove garlic, chopped or minced

1 carrot, diced

1 cup diced celery

2 cups button mushrooms, chopped

1/2 cup green bell pepper, chopped

1 cup cooked rice

1 cup cooked kasha

1 egg

Salt and pepper, to taste

Potato filling:

1/4 cup (1/2 stick) butter

3 (3 cups) yellow onions, chopped

4 cups mashed russet potatoes

Salt and pepper, to taste

Dough:

1/3 cup (about 2 eggs) egg whites

2 tablespoons vegetable oil

1/4 teaspoon salt

3/4 cups water

3 cups all-purpose flour

1 egg, well beaten, plus one teaspoon water
   for egg wash

To make the vegetable filling, heat the oil in a medium skillet. Add the onions, garlic, carrots, celery, mushrooms, and green pepper and sauté, stirring occasionally, for 10 minutes, or until the vegetables are tender. Stir in the rice, kasha, and egg. Season with salt and pepper. Remove from the heat and set it aside to cool.

To make the potato filling, in a medium skillet, heat and sauté the onion until it is golden brown. Stir in the mashed potatoes, and add salt and pepper to taste. Remove from the heat and set it aside to cool.

To make the dough, combine the egg whites, 2 tablespoons of the oil, salt, water, and flour and beat with an electric mixer on medium speed until it is smooth. Pour a thin layer of oil over the dough. Let it stand at room temperature for 1 hour.

Preheat the oven to 350 degrees.

To make the knishes, knead the dough on a heavily floured board until smooth and elastic, about 5 minutes. Roll out to 1/8-inch thick, shaping into a 14 x 24-inch oblong pan. Brush the dough with oil. Spoon the potato filling along one long edge of the dough. Spoon the vegetable filling along the other long edge. Roll the dough over the filling and continue rolling toward the center. Then roll the other side toward the center in the same way. Separate the 2 rolls by cutting down the center. Cut each roll crosswise into 2 pieces. Place all 4 pieces on a heavily greased baking sheet. Brush them with oil and bake for 35 to 40 minutes, or until they are golden brown. Remove from the oven and brush with egg wash. Return to the oven and bake 10 minutes longer. Cut it into 1 1/2-inch pieces and serve it warm. Or let it cool, slice it, wrap it in aluminum foil and freeze for up to 12 months to use when desired.

Serves 4 (4 knishes)

Russ & Daughters Appetizing Store

You can't talk about deli food without speaking of this nearly century-old culinary landmark. But whatever you do, don't call Russ & Daughters Appetizing Store a deli. It is a traditional "appetizing store," selling only dairy and fish. Meat is not sold here. The store is located in the same location, a former tenement building listed on the National Historic Registry, since the 1920s. This immaculate, white-tiled, smoked fish emporium, presided over by countermen in white coats, sells the silkiest, most glistening smoked fish south of 14th Street.

Only three items were available when Russ & Daughters first opened: salt-cured lox, pickles cured in a barrel, and schmaltz herring. Today you'll find whitefish, sturgeon, sable, herring fillets in mustard dill or lemon ginger sauce, Swedish matjes herring, Icelandic schmaltz fillets, German roll-mops, Holland herring, Scottish salmon, wild Pacific king salmon, Gaspe salmon, gravlax, and salmon tartare.

It all began in 1900 when Joel Russ started his pushcart business, delivering herring. Fourteen years later, Joel and his wife, Bella, opened a storefront on Orchard Street. The successful business moved to its present location on Houston Street in the 1920s. When Joel discovered that his daughters had more charm than he did, he expanded the name of his store to include them, and history was made on this busy street in the Lower East Side of New York City.

At Russ & Daughters Appetizing Store, be ready to stand in line — the lines typically run out the door — and since there is no table seating, be prepared to take your food home. If you have questions, ask Herman, the Yiddish-speaking Dominican man who is always there to help. An expert on all things fish, Herman is known as the fish maven whose knowledge and good service is right along the lines of what New Yorkers have come to expect from this steadfast specialty store.

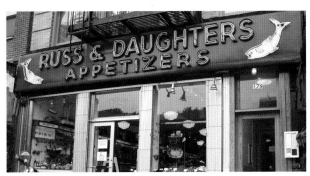

Photo, 2001. (Courtesy of Joshua Tupper)

Russ & Daughters Appetizing Store Salmon Gefilte Fish

3 1/4 pounds fresh whitefish

7 pounds fresh salmon

3 3/4 yellow onions, thickly sliced

6 eggs, beaten

1/2 cup kosher salt

1/8 cup sugar

1/2 cup matzo meal

1/2 cup finely chopped fresh dill

1 teaspoon black pepper

1/4 cup seltzer

Fish stock:

1 1/2 pounds fish bones

1/2 yellow onion, cut into quarters

1 celery stalk, including leaves

1/8 cup flat-leaf parsley, chopped, including stems

1/2 teaspoon dried thyme

1 bay leaf

1/4 tablespoon white peppercorns

1/2 tablespoon kosher salt

2 quarts water

1/2 carrot, peeled

1/4 teaspoon sugar

1/4 cup white wine (Chardonnay is good) or
    white wine vinegar

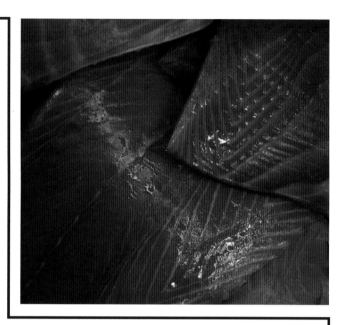

To make the gefilte fish, grind the fish with the onions using a meat grinder. Mix in the remaining ingredients. Put the mixture in the refrigerator to chill overnight. With oiled hands, shape the mixture into six 8-ounce oval patties.

Prepare the fish stock. Wash the bones in cold water to remove any scales or unwanted materials, and then combine all the ingredients in a large pot. Quickly bring it to a boil, then lower the heat to a slow simmer and cook for 1 hour, occasionally using a slotted spoon to skim off any impurities that rise to the surface. Do not allow it to boil or you will have a cloudy stock. Remove the pot from the heat; pour the stock through a fine-mesh sieve lined with cheesecloth. Cover the stock container and place in the refrigerator at once so that the stock can thicken and become gelatinous. (The fish stock may be made ahead and kept refrigerated for up to 1 week. It can also be kept frozen for as long as 6 months.)

Place the fish patties in the simmering fish stock. Cover loosely and simmer for 20 to 30 minutes, or until gefilte fish is firm to the touch and slightly paler in color than the original pink. When the gefilte fish is cooked, remove it from the water and let it cool for 15 minutes. Use a spoon to remove the gefilte fish, and serve.

Serves 10 to 12

Photo, 2003. The savory smoked salmon at Russ & Daughters is pink and orange and always hand sliced. *(Courtesy of Allison Firor)*

Russ & Daughters Appetizing Store Sour Cream Sauce

2 cups sour cream

1/2 cup buttermilk

2 tablespoons marinade from pickled lox (see below)

In a glass bowl, place the sour cream, buttermilk, and marinade. Mix well. If it is too thick, add a little more buttermilk.

Makes 2 1/2 cups

Russ & Daughters Appetizing Store Pickled Lox

2 pounds salt-cured wild Pacific salmon (belly lox)

2 large onions, peeled and sliced into rounds

5 cups cold water

1 cup white vinegar

1 cup sugar

1/2 cup mixed pickling spices, including coriander seed, mustard seed, dill, seed, allspice, bay leaf, and dried chile pepper in equal amounts

Place the lox in a pan deep enough to cover the lox with water comfortably. Soak the lox overnight in water in the refrigerator, changing the water once. Cut the lox pieces into half-pound chunks. Place them in a glass bowl, layering them with onion slices. In a mixing bowl, place the 5 cups water, vinegar, sugar, and mixed pickling spices. Stir the mixture until the sugar dissolves. Pour the mixture over the salmon, cover, and leave it at room temperature overnight so that the pickling process starts. In the morning, place it in the refrigerator and let it marinate for at least 2 days, or until it is ready to use. Reserve 2 tablespoons of the marinade to make Russ & Daughters Appetizing Store Sour Cream Sauce (see above). Serve the lox as is or with the Sour Cream Sauce.

Serves 8

Schnider's Delicatessen

The sign behind the counter at Schnider's Delicatessen reads "Hot Postroma," spelled the way it was spelled in the early part of the twentieth century. Opening in 1919 on the site of a former candy store, Schnider's thrived in Springfield, Massachusetts, for 50 years.

Jacob Schnider emigrated from Lithuania at the age of 18. When he married, he and his wife, Rose, decided they would make a living as deli owners. They spent their honeymoon setting up their new store.

In typical deli fashion, Schnider's Delicatessen was mostly counter service, with only one table, a few chairs, barrels of pickles and herring in the front, and sawdust on the floor. It was a classic delicatessen of the era between 1919 and 1971, and was also the only delicatessen in the entire Springfield area. Schnider's was known throughout New England for its homemade, hand-cut corned beef, tongue, pastrami, and hard-to-find specialty canned goods. Patrons came from all over New England, from Maine to Connecticut, to purchase their kosher provisions.

Schnider's Delicatessen closed in 1971, taking its recipes with it. One patron, Arthur Fiedler, the conductor of the Boston Pops Orchestra for fifty years, dined there often, and was loyal through the very last days the beloved delicatessen was in business.

Stage Deli

The cultural essence of New York is in its individual parts, and the sights, sounds, and smells of New York City are the reasons one goes to the Stage Deli.

The Stage Deli takes its name in part from the city's glittering past. It is a place where the stars from stage, screen, and vaudeville congregated. Something like an old dowager, today it still commands respect and love.

In 1937 Russian immigrant Max Asnas opened a small deli on the corner of Broadway and 48th Street. The location was excellent, surrounded on all sides by theaters, and actors, comedians, and theatergoers came in at all hours for his famous sandwiches. Max lost his lease in 1943 and had to relocate to his present location at 7th Avenue and 54th Street. Within nine years the deli expanded to accommodate eighty-one seats. Nothing but the location changed, and the loyal clientele from all walks of show business stayed true to the Stage. Walter Winchell was a regular and occasionally dropped a plug for the deli in his column, calling Max Asnas "the Corned Beef Confucius." Though sometimes a bit gruff, Max was the epitome of a deli owner, with a quick wit, stocky build, and thick accent; he won the respect of all who met him.

Max Asnas was the first to name a deli sandwich after a celebrity. Stars came in and built a sandwich just as they liked it, and Max added it to the menu. Celebrities today still covet a place on a deli menu as the ultimate status symbol. There are newer creations like the Tom Cruise (roast beef, turkey or brisket, with gravy and fries) and the Dolly Parton (pastrami and corned beef on twin rolls), but make no mistake: it's the meat that brings in the patrons. The ambience keeps them there.

Story has it that the evening the Beatles were to appear in their first U.S. performance, on *The Ed Sullivan Show*, the four performers came to the Stage Deli for dinner. As they looked somewhat disheveled and slightly unkempt, Asnas was suspicious at first and refused to let them in the restaurant. Wisely, he relented, they had dinner, and the rest is history!

Stage Deli Cheese Blintzes

Crêpe batter:

3 large eggs

1/4 cup water

1/4 cup milk

1/2 teaspoon baking powder

1/2 cup all-purpose flour

1 1/2 teaspoons sugar

1 tablespoon unsalted butter

2 tablespoons vegetable oil

Filling:

1 1/2 cups farmer cheese

2 cups pot-style cottage cheese

1/4 cup sugar

1/4 teaspoon pure vanilla extract

1 large egg

1 tablespoon all-purpose flour

1 1/2 teaspoons ground cinnamon (optional)

Sour cream, for serving

Confectioners' sugar, for dusting

Assorted preserves, for serving (optional)

To make the crêpes, combine the eggs, water, milk, baking powder, flour, and sugar in a blender and refrigerate for 30 minutes. In an 8-inch nonstick skillet, melt half of the butter over moderately high heat. Pour in enough batter to just coat the bottom of skillet, swirling and cooking undisturbed until the top is set and the bottom is golden when gently lifted at the edge (do not flip). Transfer the crêpes to paper towels in a single layer, golden side down. Repeat process with the remaining butter and batter until all is used.

To make the filling, in a food processor fitted with the metal blade, blend the cheeses, sugar, vanilla, and egg until the mixture is not quite smooth (do not overblend). If necessary, add more flour in small increments to thicken it.

To make the blintzes, with the golden side of the blintz wrapper facing down, put 3 tablespoons of filling in the center of each wrapper and fold the opposite sides over the filling until the sides barely touch. Fold in the ends to completely enclose the filling, forming packets, and arrange the blintzes seam side down on a baking sheet. Repeat with the remaining filling and wrappers. Heat 1 tablespoon of vegetable oil in a large skillet over medium heat. Place 5 blintzes in a frying pan, seam side down. Sauté them until browned and heated through, about 2 minutes per side. Repeat with the remaining blintzes. Serve them plain, topped with sour cream and sprinkled with confectioners' sugar, or with assorted fruit spreads.

Serves 4 (8 to 10 blintzes)

Stage Deli Potato Latkes

4 (2 pounds) russet potatoes, peeled and cubed

2 large eggs

1 small yellow onion, finely grated

1/3 cup matzo meal

Salt and pepper to taste

Vegetable oil, for frying

Sour cream, for serving

Applesauce, for serving

Grind the potatoes in a grinder or pulse until they are finely chopped in a food processor fitted with the metal blade. Transfer them to a strainer set over a large bowl and drain well. Discard the liquid.

Preheat the oven to 200 degrees.

In a large mixing bowl, whisk the eggs. Add the potatoes and onions and mix them to combine. Add the matzo meal and stir it to blend. Season with salt and pepper.

Pour the oil into a large skillet to the depth of 1/4 inch. Heat the oil on medium heat until it begins to bubble on the surface. Working in batches, drop the potato mixture into the skillet by 1/4 cupfuls. Use a spatula to flatten them into 3-inch-diameter pancakes. Cook them until brown and crisp, about 5 minutes per side. Transfer pancakes to paper towels to drain. Keep them warm in a preheated oven while you cook the remaining potato pancakes. Serve warm with sour cream or applesauce.

Serves 10 to 12 (20 to 22 latkes)

Stage Deli Cheesecake

4 tablespoons graham cracker crumbs

4 (8-ounce) packages cream cheese,
   at room temperature

1 cup sugar

4 eggs

1/2 teaspoon pure vanilla extract

Fresh strawberries or blueberries or
   favorite preserves for serving (optional)

Preheat the oven to 325 degrees.

Sprinkle the bottom of a lightly greased, 9-inch springform pan with graham cracker crumbs. Combine the cheese and sugar in a blender or with an electric mixer at medium speed until they are well mixed. Add the eggs, one at a time, mixing well after each addition. Blend in the vanilla. Pour the mixture into the springform pan, wrapping the bottom and sides of the pan tightly with aluminum foil. Place the springform pan in a large roasting pan. Add enough hot water to come halfway up the sides of the springform pan. Bake for 50 to 60 minutes, or until a toothpick inserted into the center of the cheesecake comes out clean.

Cool the cake in the pan on a wire rack. When it is cool, loosen the cake from the rim of the pan using the blade of a knife. If desired, top it with fresh fruit — strawberries or blueberries — or fruit preserves. Refrigerate the cheesecake until you are ready to serve it.

Serves 12

Photo, circa 1952. The newly refurbished Stage Deli grew to 81 seats in the early 1950s. *(Courtesy of Stage Deli)*

YONAH SHIMMEL..
.KNISH BAKERY

The Original
YONAH SCHIMMEL
KNISHERY

Yonah Schimmel Knishes

It's like going back in time when you enter Yonah Schimmel Knishes, circa 1910. This is old New York.

When Rabbi Yonah Schimmel arrived in New York City from Eastern Europe, he could not afford to support his family on the salary he earned from teaching Hebrew school. So he supplemented his income by selling knishes from a pushcart in the Lower East Side. Years later, when he was able to open a knishery, he set up shop at 137 East Houston Street near Second Avenue. This street was once known as "knish alley." The knishery stands in the very same location today.

Nothing here has changed, from the original tin ceiling to the century-old food cases, to the focal point of this eatery, the knish dumbwaiter. This creaky elevator brings the fresh-baked knishes from the basement kitchen where they are hand-rolled and baked in a 100-year-old brick oven.

Yonah Schimmel Knishes is one of the few knisheries left in the United States. Here you can reminisce and imagine what it must have been like back in the early part of the twentieth century.

Take a seat at one of the long Formica tables, close your eyes, and listen to the sound of the knish elevator slowly squeaking its way up to the floor carrying the freshly baked knishes. When you smell the dough wrapped around the tasty fillings, you are transported back to 1910.

Had you lived in the neighborhood back then, you would have come here for the one and only knish available at that time, the potato knish. No exact recipes for these knishes exist, but there are three guidelines to the special knish served here: The knish must be baked, not fried; it must be hand-rolled, not machine-rolled; and it can only be filled with the freshest ingredients.

Today you'll find not only the potato knish, but kasha, red cabbage, mushroom, broccoli, vegetable, spinach, and sweet potato knishes. There are even fruit and cheese knishes as well as chocolate knishes for dessert. Borscht is served by the glass — this is very Old World — and you can get blintzes, strudel, rugelach, and homemade yogurt. Take a trip down memory lane with Yonah Schimmel; have a knish!

Photo, 1990. The exterior of Yonah Schimmel Knish Bakery remains completely unchanged since 1910, complete with the original sign painter's misspelling of Schimmel. *(Courtesy of Yonah Schimmel Knishes)*

Yonah Schimmel-Inspired Potato Knish

This is not the original recipe but an acceptable likeness based on the author's recollection.

Potato filling:
2 russet potatoes
3/4 cup finely chopped yellow onions
2 tablespoons vegetable oil
3/4 teaspoon salt
1/8 teaspoon white pepper

Dough:
3 cups sifted all-purpose flour
1 teaspoon baking powder
1/2 teaspoon salt
1 cup water
1 egg, slightly beaten, plus 1 egg beaten
   with 1 teaspoon water for egg wash
Vegetable oil

To make the filling, peel and boil the potatoes, until they are soft. Drain the potatoes and mash them. Sauté the onions in 1 tablespoon of oil, until they are brown. Mix the potatoes, onions, salt, and pepper.

To make the dough, put the flour, baking powder, and salt into a large bowl. Add the water, egg, and 1 tablespoon of the oil. Stir with a wooden spoon until the dough holds together. Turn it out onto a lightly floured work surface. Knead it until it is smooth and elastic, using only enough dough to keep it from sticking to the board. Place the dough on a lightly floured surface, cover it with a clean kitchen towel, and let it rise for 30 minutes at room temperature.

Preheat the oven to 350 degrees. Lightly grease a baking sheet.

To make the knishes, divide the dough into 4 pieces and roll each piece into a 12-inch square. With a sharp knife, cut each piece in half to make two 6-inch-wide strips. Brush lightly with the oil and spoon some of the filling into the center. Bring one side of the pastry over the filling, roll it up to enclose completely and pinch the ends together. Place the knishes seam side down on a baking sheet. Lightly score each with a blunt knife at 1-inch intervals and brush with egg wash. Bake the knishes at 350 degrees for 30 minutes, or until they are golden.

Serves 8 (8 knishes)

Photo, date unknown. Gottlieb's Kosher Delicatessen began in the late 1800s on Duffy and Whitaker streets in Savannah, Georgia. It has been closed for many years, but it was an extremely popular deli in its day. *(Courtesy of Savannah Jewish Archives and Georgia Historical Society, Savannah, Georgia)*

Kosher Cajun Deli

Some nod must be given to this deli in New Orleans, as the South has such a short list of delis. And a kosher one at that! Owners Joel and Natalie Brown saw the need for a Jewish deli in their hometown of Metairie, Louisiana, a suburb of New Orleans. New Orleans is home to one of the oldest synagogues in America, but until this deli opened in 1987, there were no Jewish delis in the state of Louisiana. One can only imagine!

One of the trademarks of a good deli — the basket of pickles along with pickled green tomatoes, sweet kosher pickle rounds, and sour red bell peppers — is a standard at Kosher Cajun Deli. But you'll also find foods with a local flavor. The deli makes a mean kosher jambalaya, just like your grandmother might have made in the old country had cayenne pepper been available! The Cajun aspect, however, appears mostly in the regional specials. The reason to dine here is still the regular deli fare, based on a New York-style deli menu. Hungry for deli food, people now travel from Alabama, Mississippi, and Texas to Metairie to bring it home.

In August of 2005, Hurricane Katrina took its toll on the coast of Louisiana and the Kosher Cajun Deli as well, but within three months the deli was once again ready for business.

Logo, 1987. *(Courtesy of Kosher Cajun Deli)*

Photo, circa 1927. Street vendors Abe and Juda Javetz at the Savannah City Market in 1927. The Javetz family was in the meat business and sold to wholesalers and food vendors throughout Savannah, Georgia. This was a popular market for Jewish businesses before it was demolished in 1954. *(Courtesy of Savannah Jewish Archives and Georgia Historical Society, Savannah, Georgia)*

Kosher Cajun Deli Stuffed Cabbage

1 head cabbage

5 pounds ground beef

4 yellow onions, chopped

2 cloves garlic

4 bunches green onions, chopped

1 cup fresh parsley

Salt and pepper, to taste

Cayenne pepper, to taste

Cajun seasoning, to taste

2 tablespoons Italian seasoning

2 green bell peppers, finely chopped

4 celery stalks, chopped

2 cups unseasoned bread crumbs

8 cups white rice, cooked

Preheat the oven to 350 degrees.

Blanch the cabbage for 15 to 20 minutes, then break the leaves off and set them aside.

Brown the ground beef in a sauté pan. Add the onion, garlic, green onion, parsley, salt, pepper, cayenne, and Cajun seasoning. Mix well. Add the Italian seasoning, bell pepper, and celery, and stir well. Add the bread crumbs and rice.

Spread a cabbage leaf on a work surface and put 1/4 cup of the filling into it. Roll the leaf tightly to enclose and secure the filling. Place the rolls seam side down in a 15 x 12-inch roasting pan and bake them for 30 minutes. Remove the rolls from pan and serve.

Serves 10 to 12 (20 to 24 rolls)

Kosher Cajun Deli Split Pea Soup

3 cups dried split peas

2 garlic cloves, crushed

3 yellow onions, chopped

12 to 16 cups chicken broth

Salt and pepper, to taste

1/4 cup fresh parsley

Mix all the ingredients together in a pot. Bring the mixture to a boil over high heat, then lower the heat to simmer, covered, for 1 1/2 hours.

Serves 10 to 12 (1 gallon)

COKE, ROOT BEER, 7 UP, DR. PEPPER	.15
TEA OR COFFEE	.15
MILK OR CHOCOLATE MILK	.20
HOT CHOCOLATE	.25
VERNOR GINGERALE	.25
DOMESTIC BEER	.50
LOWENBRAU, light or dark (Germany's finest)	.75
HEINEKEN'S (Holland's Pride)	.75
LOWENBRAU, light, draft	.70
MICHELOB	.60

THE intention of the Olde-Tyme Delicatessen is to turn back the hands of time! Back to that era:

. . . where every man's word was his bond;

. . . where every dollar purchased quality merchandise;

. . . where every customer deserved and received courtesy and service;

. . . Our purpose is not to be critical of the rush and zoom of the Twentieth Century; but to recreate, in the midst of the hustle and bustle of mass merchandising, in some small measure—the years of yesterday. This replica of an old-time Williamsburg store is for those who wish to browse in leisure, shop with discrimination, dine on quality foods, and take advantage of the sincerely proffered commodity called "personal service."

. . . Not an empty gesture at the past, the Olde-Tyme Delicatessen is a solid promise to the future—a promise that you, our customer, shall have the service, courtesy, and quality you rightfully deserve.

So . . . let's turn back the clock! Turn back the hours. Pleasant shopping. The best of eating! Where the hands of the clock, and the hands of everyone in this establishment, are dedicated to . . . making the "tyme" you spend here satisfying . . .

Menu, 1961. A interior portion of the original menu from the Olde Tyme Deli. *(Courtesy of Irving Feldman)*

Olde Tyme Deli

Who would have thought to have a Jewish deli in the middle of Mississippi? New Yorkers Irv and Judy Feldman did. Before Irv and Judy opened the Olde Tyme Deli in Jackson in 1961, there was no other way to buy the foods that local people needed for the holidays. The opening of their deli met with great success.

The Feldmans had a dream when they moved to Jackson in the early 1960s. That dream was to open a deli in which they would maintain quality and have a good family atmosphere. It would be a place where they knew all the customers' names. But serving the community in Jackson was different than it would have been in New York or Los Angeles; here they had to be a jack of all trades. They had to try to please many diverse palates.

Locals were not used to a New York-style deli, but with the arrival of civil rights workers and their desire for deli food, locals of Jackson began to appreciate bagels and lox, pastrami, and cheese blintzes. The Olde Tyme Deli's food was fresh, its breads and pastries were baked on the premises, and with the exception of a few unorthodox Southern items on the menu, like gumbo and red beans and rice, it was in all senses of the word a deli, albeit a Southern Jewish deli.

This era was not without controversy; civil rights workers found themselves dining beside members of the Ku Klux Klan. These Klan members hoped to influence Mr. Feldman in the manner in which they thought the deli should be run. That never happened, and the Feldmans continued to hold the respect of the entire community. When the Olde Tyme Deli closed in 1996, its recipes went with it and left a huge hole in the heart of the South.

WE'RE TURNING THE CLOCK BACK TO QUALITY

Olde Tyme
DELICATESSEN

Menu, 1961. *(Courtesy of Irving Feldman)*

. . . Entertaining with cards? O
SPECIALS are your "ace" for excell

...For Kings

Olde-Tyme's "Royal Flush" (beat
going!)—Treat your poker party to
tween a delicatessen pizza and a
loaf of freshly-baked Italian Sesar
assortment of Kosher corned beef,
and sliced turkey, cut into six m
yourself to this new and different
six

(Potato Salad or Cole Slaw Ava

...For Queens

Trumps for your "Club" — Olde-
Special: Patio chix salad garnished
fancy "frosted" potato salad; an
Dessert tray of apple strudel and le
designed for a minimum of eight

(Pick out your bridge prize from ou
sweets and imported delicacies.)

-in-a-Wheel

more, anytime, anywhere — Lazy
ple portions of artfully arranged lay

eef	Ham
heese	Swiss Cheese
	Salami
lad	

Minimum order of six persons to
here!

-Tyme Box Lunch

You Are!

lunch time! Take one out to the
ch supper; family reunion; or you

BOX-LUNCH — Kosher corned b
; potato chips; crisp "new" Kosh
essert

BOX-LUNCH — Slo-baked coun
potato chips; "new" Kosher pick

MIDWEST

Menu art, 1956. *(Courtesy of Corky & Lenny's)*

Corky & Lenny's

In a suburb of Cleveland, Ohio, sits a deli that is one of the last longstanding Eastern European-style Jewish delis in the Midwest. Originally opened by Sanford (Corky) Kurland and Leonard (Lenny) Kaden in 1956, Corky & Lenny's was long known for its chocolate phosphate — the New York-style egg cream. What remains to this day is a newly renovated, Art Deco–styled deli with new owners and a terrific matzo ball soup featuring football-sized matzo balls! (The mushroom barley soup isn't too bad either.) Well-known patrons like former New York Mayor Ed Koch, actors Debra Winger and Chad Douglas, and the famous deli fresser Jackie Mason are among those who regularly enjoy the menu's culinary feats.

Corky & Lenny's is a good example of how, if deli owners make sure to pass the torch, a cherished tradition can continue for a very long time.

Corky & Lenny's Stuffed Cabbage

1 yellow onion, chopped

8 cups tomato puree

1 (6-ounce) can tomato paste

Sugar, to taste

Salt and pepper, to taste

Garlic powder, to taste

2 pounds ground beef

2 eggs

1/2 cup ketchup

1/2 cup uncooked rice

1 large green cabbage, cored

1 quart sauerkraut, drained

Preheat the oven to 350 degrees.

Brown onions in sauté pan until soft. Add tomato sauce and paste. Add sugar, salt, pepper, and garlic powder. Cover pan and simmer for 1 hour.

Place the ground beef in a bowl; add the salt, pepper, garlic powder, eggs, ketchup, and rice, and blend the beef mixture with a spoon until it is pasty. Cook the cabbage in boiling water for 20 minutes. Remove it from water and peel off the leaves one at a time, being careful not to tear them. (Be sure leaves are soft before you remove them.) Cut off the hardcores on each leaf. Place the leaves flat on the counter and fill each with a small handful of meat in the center. Cover the meat with a flap of cabbage and fold in the corners. Roll the cabbage leaf until it completely covers the meat. Repeat until all the meat and cabbage leaves are used.

Place the stuffed cabbage in a pan, spread 1 tablespoon of sauerkraut on top of each, and cover them completely with sauce. Cover the pan with aluminum foil and bake for 30 to 60 minutes.

Serves 7 to 15 (15 rolls)

CRISCO RECIPES
for the JEWISH HOUSEWIFE

Cookbook cover, 1933. *(Courtesy of Proctor & Gamble)*

Photo, circa 1915. *(Courtesy of Collectors Press, Inc.)*

Menu, 1956. *(Courtesy of Corky & Lenny's)*

Corky & Lenny's Chopped Liver

1 pound chicken livers

2 medium yellow onions, chopped

1/2 cup vegetable oil, plus more as needed

2 hard-boiled eggs

Salt and pepper, to taste

Preheat the oven to 350 degrees.

Cook the chicken livers on top of the stove in an ovenproof skillet until they are brown on the outside. Place them in the oven and bake for 30 minutes. Allow the livers to cool. Sauté the onions in the oil until they are soft and brown. Set them aside to cool.

Place the chicken livers, eggs, and onion mixture in a coarse meat grinder or in the bowl of a food processor fitted with the metal blade. Add salt and pepper and mix. If the mixture is dry, add more vegetable oil.

Serves 10

Darbys and Boesky's

Though now long shuttered, this deli, an icon in the lives of Detroiters, was the place to meet, eat, and greet. Owned and operated by Sam Boesky, Boesky's Delicatessen and Darbys were two of the most well known delicatessens in America.

Sam Boesky emigrated from Russia to Detroit, Michigan, in 1913. Unable to read or write English, he worked on a milk route while planning his first deli. Opening Boesky's Delicatessen in 1917 in a former candy store on Hastings Street and Farnsworth Avenue (the heart of a then-thriving Jewish neighborhood) at just seventeen years of age was a testament to Sam's dedication to making it in America. But he was a risk taker, and although the deli was extremely popular, he sold it in 1923, just six years later. Sam went on to open and close other smaller delis, and he even left the restaurant business for a stint in the construction trade. But in 1955, he devised an idea for a deli/restaurant that would become one of the great showplaces of the Midwest.

It was here, on 7 Mile Road in Detroit, Michigan, that Darbys was conceived. With help from friends and investors, Sam opened Darbys (a name he picked out of a hat) in January 1956. The day it opened, the lines were so long the kitchen almost ran out of food. The doors were locked to keep the crowds to a minimum, and no one was allowed into Darbys until someone left. Anytime of the day or night, you could be assured of meeting friends,

local celebrities, or politicians. No place has ever reached the status this deli had and sadly will never see again. In the true sense of a deli, this was a home away from home.

Some of the appeal of Darbys was that the deli fare was more sophisticated than the usual corned beef and chopped liver sandwiches. A special dining room along with a private banquet room and cocktail lounge made this a spot for more than just deli foods. Here, they featured a nightly menu offering such items as the popular chicken poulet and broiled fresh lake whitefish. But at lunch, it was the sumptuous sandwiches, from chopped liver to the most mouthwatering pastrami in town, that brought in the crowds.

Sam Boesky was committed to offering his customers the best food and the best service. His motto was "The customer comes first." He served nearly 4,300 people daily with the help of 120 employees, and all the pastries were baked on the premises. This wasn't just a local neighborhood delicatessen; it had a reputation across the United States.

On July 15, 1968, Darbys burned to the ground. To the many patrons, waitresses, cooks, and bakers, it was the end of an era. Their treasured meeting place for the best food in town was no more. Darby's never reopened, and those extraordinary times are nothing more than a distant memory.

Top left and right: Menu art, 1956. *(Courtesy of Rhonda Kerner)*

DARBYS

DARBYS HAS NO AFFILIATION WITH ANY OTHER RESTAURANT

"The best of food ... with the best of people

PROPRIETOR, SAM BOBS

Darbys Chicken Poulet

This is not the original Darbys Chicken Poulet recipe, but it has been tested and revised based on the author's memory of the original.

1/2 stick unsalted butter, clarified

1/2 medium-size yellow onion, minced

1/4 cup all-purpose flour

2 1/2 cups milk

Pinch of salt

Pinch of freshly ground white pepper

Pinch of freshly grated nutmeg

Sprig of fresh thyme

2 egg yolks, lightly beaten

1/2 cup freshly grated Parmesan or
    Gruyère cheese, plus extra for topping

2 tablespoons unsalted butter, divided

4 tablespoons whipping cream

4 pieces lightly toasted white bread

4 boneless chicken breasts, poached

To make the béchamel sauce, heat the clarified butter in a heavy saucepan over low heat. Add the onion and cook until it is translucent. Add the flour and continue to cook over low heat, stirring constantly to form a roux. Remove the pan from the heat and set it aside.

In a separate saucepan, bring the milk to a boil over medium-high heat. Whisk the roux into the milk and continue to whisk until it is smoothly blended. Add the salt, white pepper, nutmeg, and thyme and simmer gently for 30 minutes, stirring often until the sauce is thick and smooth.

Maintaining low heat, add the egg yolks, slowly stirring until they are blended. Just as the sauce is about to boil, remove the pan from the heat. (If the sauce boils it will curdle.) Add the cheese and 1 tablespoon of butter and stir the sauce until thoroughly combined.

When you are ready to serve, whip the cream in a mixer on high speed until it forms soft peaks; fold into the sauce. Grease 4 oval ramekins with the remaining tablespoon of butter. Place the bread on the bottom of the ramekins, add the chicken breasts, smother with the sauce, and sprinkle with some cheese. Place the dish under the broiler and cook until it is nicely browned and bubbling on top, about 2 to 3 minutes. The sauce yields approximately 3 cups.

Serves 4 (4 chicken breasts)

Protzel's Delicatessen

A secret was imparted to Bob Protzel in 1956 that was to be kept until a young and deserving deli successor would someday come along. It was a recipe for corned beef that proved to be the best corned beef anywhere. This "secret" was passed on to the Protzel's sons, Alan and Ronnie, and now to grandson Max, and the exact ingredients will continue to remain in the family.

When Bob and Evelyn Protzel opened this unassuming deli in 1954 in a suburb of St. Louis, Missouri, their goal was to provide a good living for their family. If success were to come, that would be a plus. Working very hard and preparing everything from scratch was their motto. They made their own gefilte fish, pickled their own pickles and even ground fresh horseradish. Everything they served had to be fresh and pure.

Protzel's Delicatessen has become a landmark of sorts for this midwestern town. The location has been the same for over fifty years and few changes have been made. There are still no menus. The shelves still contain the same special mustards and delicacies, and the bakery cases are filled with fresh bagels, breads, cookies, and mandelbrot. Deli cases overflow with homemade potato salad, a house specialty, knishes, kugels, and their well-known

and loved chopped chicken liver. But penny candy is no longer sold here, the horseradish is no longer ground in the kitchen, and there is now counter seating for patrons. The sign over the counter reads "Diet and Lean are four-letter words."

A salami that was framed the day Protzel's opened still hangs in the deli, along with one from 2004, as the torch was passed to the third generation of the Protzel family. Framed and hanging above the meat counter, it's a constant reminder of the tradition that has followed in this family-owned delicatessen.

Protzel's Delicatessen Chopped Liver

1 pound chicken livers

1 small yellow onion, sliced

3 hard-boiled eggs

Salt and pepper, to taste

1/4 cup vegetable oil or schmaltz (chicken fat)

Broil the liver just until it is done, about 15 minutes over medium heat. In a separate pan, add the schmaltz or oil and sauté the onion until golden. Do not overcook. Put the liver, eggs, and onion in a food processor and process on the pulse setting until the mixture is smooth. Place it in a bowl and add salt, pepper, and schmaltz or oil. Beat the mixture until it is smooth and fluffy. Serve the chopped liver as an appetizer or in a sandwich. It can also be molded.

Serves 8

Photo, 1954. Opening day at Protzel's Delicatessen, with Bob Protzel behind the counter and ready for business. *(Courtesy of Alan Protzel)*

- 134 -

Shapiro's Delicatessen

The food business was in Louis Shapiro's blood, as his grandfather had been the primary food supplier to the czar's navel fleet in Russia. Louis Shapiro always aspired to live in America. Even while living in Odessa, Russia, he owned and operated the American Grocery Company. Coming to America in 1903, he headed for the heartland of Indiana in hopes of joining a friend in the scrap business. That venture lasted only three weeks. At that point, he and his wife, Rebecca, decided to peddle tea and coffee from a horse-drawn wagon. By 1905 they were able to purchase a small building on the corner of Meridian and McCarty Streets in Southern Indianapolis, where on the lower level he opened Shapiro's Grocery and Deli. He and his wife, and eventually their eight children, would reside on the top floor of that building, which remains intact to this day.

As years passed, Louis Shapiro primarily sold canned goods as well as pickles and deli meats, and when Prohibition ended in 1933, his business began picking up for deli sandwiches and beer. This would begin the transition from a grocery business to a delicatessen.

"We're all products of the people who came before us, and the wisdom they pass down." These words are from the advertisement long used by the deli, and the words hold true today. Of the eight children, four went into the deli business with their father. Today, Brian Shapiro, a fourth-generation great-grandson, is at the counter serving at least 2,000 people weekly. Known for its potato pancakes, sour cream egg noodles, baked chicken, and stuffed cabbage, the deli has expanded to accommodate up to 250 people.

Dispensing 300 pounds of corned beef, 100 pounds of pastrami, turkey, roast beef, and 200 loaves of

---

Shapiro's Delicatessen New York Style Cheesecake

Graham cracker crust:

3/4 cup graham cracker crumbs

1/4 cup sugar

4 tablespoons margarine or butter, melted

Dash of pure vanilla extract

Cheese filling:

3 1/2 pounds cream cheese

1 1/4 cups sugar

1 tablespoon freshly squeezed lemon juice

1/2 tablespoon pure vanilla extract

8 extra large eggs, beaten

To make the crust, mix all of the ingredients in a large bowl and press the mixture into an 8-inch round cake pan. Set aside.

Preheat the oven to 350 degrees.

Using an electric mixer, use medium to high speed to beat the cream cheese, sugar, lemon juice, and vanilla, adding eggs one at a time as you mix. Pour the finished mixture into the graham cracker crust. Place the cake pan in a water bath — a roasting pan filled with 2 inches of water — and bake it in the oven for 2 hours.

Chill, serve, eat, and enjoy!

Serves 8 to 10

---

fresh breads is a lot of food to manage on a daily basis, but as Louis Shapiro always said, "Cook good, serve generous, price modestly, and people will come." And they do!

Opposite page: (Top) Photo, 1930s. The original Shapiro's Delicatessen with some 1930s Art Deco modification. (Below) Photo, 1940. Louis Shapiro's son Max beside a display of horseradish, mustard, and catsup that were sold with other standard deli fare in his delicatessen.
(Courtesy of Shapiro's Delicatessen)

Shapiro's Delicatessen
Hot German Potato Salad

1/8 cup apple cider vinegar

2 tablespoons sugar

1/2 tablespoon salt

1 cup water

1/2 pound corned beef

Vegetable oil

Pepper, to taste

2 tablespoons yellow mustard

1/4 cup chopped lettuce

3 pounds cooked red potatoes, peeled and sliced

Make a vinegar base by heating the apple cider vinegar in a small saucepan over medium heat with the sugar and salt. When the sugar is dissolved, add the water. Set aside.

Put the corned beef in the bowl of a food processor fitted with the metal blade and chop or grind the meat. Transfer the mixture to a 2-quart pan with a little oil and a pinch or two of black pepper. Add the yellow mustard, chopped lettuce, and red potatoes, and add the vinegar base. Refrigerate the salad before serving.

Serves 6 to 8 (4 pounds)

Photo, 1940. Abe Shapiro, son of Louis, proudly stands behind the counter. *(Courtesy of Shapiro's Delicatessen)*

Shapiro's Delicatessen Stuffed Cabbage

2 heads cabbage

1 pound lean ground chuck

2 medium-size onions, finely chopped

1 celery stalk, finely chopped

1 egg, beaten

3 slices white bread soaked in 1/3 cup red wine

1/4 cup tomato juice

1 cup cooked rice

1 teaspoon salt, plus more as needed

1/2 teaspoon black pepper, plus more as needed

2 cups stewed tomatoes

1/2 cup tomato purée

1 cup water

1/2 cup brown sugar

Juice of 1 lemon

6 gingersnap cookies (about 2 inches in diameter)

1/2 cup golden raisins

Core the cabbage and blanch it in a large pot of boiling water until the leaves begin to loosen.

Combine the ground chuck, onion, celery, and egg. Mix in the wet bread. (Bare hands are the best tools for this.) Add the tomato juice, rice, salt, and pepper.

Carefully peel off the cabbage leaves and roll each one around the meat mixture. Tuck in the sides so they hold together. Repeat the steps until all the beef is wrapped; there should be 18 to 20 packets. Chop the remaining cabbage leaves and reserve 4 cups.

To make the sauce, in a large stockpot, heat the stewed tomatoes, tomato purée, water, brown sugar, and lemon juice over medium heat. Crumble the gingersnaps and stir them into the mixture. Stir in the raisins and chopped cabbage leaves. Adjust the salt and pepper as desired.

Carefully add the stuffed cabbage packets to the sauce. Cover the pot and cook over medium-low heat for 1 hour and 15 minutes. Check it occasionally and add 1/4 to 1/2 cup of tomato juice to the sauce if it seems to be drying out.

Serves 6 (18 to 20 rolls)

Photo, 1993. The founders, Paul Saginaw and Ari Weinzweig, surrounded by a plethora of their Bakehouse breads. *(Courtesy of Zingerman's Delicatessen)*

Photo, 1994. *(Courtesy of Zingerman's Delicatessen)*

Zingerman's Delicatessen

Zingerman's Delicatessen isn't just a deli; it's a small empire (or, as the owners like to call it, "the coolest small company in America"). In the midwestern college town of Ann Arbor, Michigan, there is a creamery for handcrafting cheese and other dairy goodies, a mail-order business, a bakehouse that bakes all the breads and pastries, a catering business, and a restaurant, Zingerman's Delicatessen, the great deli that started it all. It is a multimillion-dollar business.

It began in the most unlikely of ways. No, this is not a third-generation family-owned business. Ari Weinzweig and Paul Saginaw, graduates of the University of Michigan with degrees in Russian history and zoology, respectively, found a niche and went all the way with it. Both grew up eating Jewish food and were frustrated not to find it anywhere in Ann Arbor. So, coupled with a food business fantasy and some knowledge of how to run a restaurant, they hit upon the name Zingerman's Delicatessen. (They wanted a Jewish-sounding name with a little zing.) It was 1982, a time when no one was opening delis, except these two. And what a deli it is.

Ann Arbor is a town with a high level of culture, and with many of Zingerman's clientele being from the East, the deli is careful not to serve inferior corned beef or pastrami. On the menu here is traditional fare such as deli meats, chopped liver, and chicken soup, as well as olive oils, olives, vinegars, and the cheeses for which Zingerman's are also famous.

Opening in a quirky orange brick building built in 1902 and now on the registry of historic buildings, Zingerman's Delicatessen looks like it's been here for years. Zingerman's is a deli, although a modern-day one with cartoons on the wall, booths, and four communal tables. And who are we to argue? This is just like a traditional deli, complete with free samples and the classic counterman banter. Its breads and sandwiches are legendary, and its fragrant Jewish rye bread is sublime. The deli's vision was for the sandwiches to be so big it would take two hands to hold them and that the sauce would roll down the forearms. When eating other sandwiches, Ari and Paul wanted people to say, "This is a great sandwich but it's not Zingerman's."

Zingerman's Delicatessen #24: The Ferber Experience

1 pound Niman Ranch or any high-quality
  pastrami, sliced
1 loaf Zingerman's pumpernickel bread
1 cup Zingerman's Delicatessen Scallion
  Cream Cheese (see right)
1 cup (8 leaves) fresh leaf lettuce

Preheat the oven to 350 degrees.

Sprinkle the pastrami with a little water, wrap it tightly in foil, and place it in the oven. At the same time, put the whole loaf of pumpernickel, unwrapped, into the oven. After 15 to 20 minutes, remove the bread from the oven — the crust should be crunchy but not overly hard. Set the bread on the counter and let it stand for 5 minutes. Remove the pastrami from the oven and set it aside, still wrapped.

As soon as the pumpernickel has cooled enough to handle it, place it on a cutting board. Hold the loaf on its side, with its top crust facing away from you, and slice it diagonally. The slices should be about the size of the palm of your hand. Cut 2 slices per sandwich. While the bread is still warm, spread each slice to the edge with 1 tablespoon of Zingerman's Delicatessen Scallion Cream Cheese.

When unwrapping the package of pastrami, be careful when releasing the hot steam. For each sandwich, pile about 4 to 5 ounces (4 slices) of the hot pastrami onto 1 slice of bread. Layer on 2 pieces of lettuce, and top with another slice of bread. Cut the sandwich in half diagonally and serve.

Serves 4 (4 sandwiches)

Zingerman's Delicatessen Scallion Cream Cheese

16 ounces handmade (non-vegetable gum)
  cream cheese (found in specialty grocery stores)
14 scallions, green parts only, chopped

Place the cream cheese in a medium bowl and gently fold in the scallions. Store in the refrigerator for up to 7 days.

Makes 16 ounces

Zingerman's Delicatessen Smoked Whitefish Salad

1 (1 1/2 pounds or 2 cups) whole smoked whitefish
2 tablespoons mayonnaise
2 tablespoons plus 2 teaspoons sour cream
2 1/2 teaspoons freshly squeezed lemon juice
2 tablespoons chopped red onion
1/4 cup finely chopped parsley, loosely packed
1 medium-size seedless cucumber, chopped

Remove the skin, bones, and any brown bits from the whitefish and discard them. Flake the fish into small pieces in a medium bowl, checking again for any bones.

In a separate medium bowl, mix together the mayonnaise, sour cream, and lemon juice. Gently stir in the onion, parsley, cucumber, and flaked fish. This is best served cold as an appetizer or side dish.

Serves 4 (about 3 1/2 cups)

Flyer, 2005. (Courtesy of Zingerman's Delicatessen

Zingerman's Events

"[Zingerman's is] the Coolest Small Company in America." Inc magazine, January 2003

Brochure art, 2005. *(Courtesy of Zingerman's Delicatessen)*

Menu, 2005. *(Courtesy of Zingerman's Delicatessen)*

Zingerman's Delicatessen Hamentaschen

The Jewish holiday Purim brings Hamentaschen — the traditional, three-cornered pastry pockets stuffed with sweet filling such as prune, apricot, strawberry, fig, or any sort of preserves you prefer.

Crust:

2/3 cup plus 4 teaspoons butter,
    at room temperature

1/2 cup sugar

1 large egg

1 1/2 teaspoons pure vanilla extract

2 1/2 cups all-purpose flour, plus more
    for rolling out dough

1 1/2 cups preserves (any type)

Preheat the oven to 350 degrees.

In a large bowl, cream the butter and sugar together at medium speed using an electric mixer. Add the egg and vanilla and combine well. Stir in the flour a little at a time. Using your hands, mix the flour and the wet ingredients until the dough forms. Shape the dough into a ball. Separate the ball into 4 parts. Set 1 piece of the dough onto a lightly floured surface, then cover the other 3 pieces with a clean kitchen towel.

Working with 1 portion of dough at a time, roll out the dough thinly, about 1/8-inch, and cut out 4 1/2-inch rounds. Set them aside or on an ungreased baking sheet. Take the leftover scraps of dough and re-roll; continue re-rolling and cutting rounds until all of the dough is used. Place a rounded tablespoon of preserves in the center of each round and fold the dough over the filling toward the center, pinching the dough together where it meets to form a triangle with a small opening in the center.

Bake the Hamentaschen on an ungreased baking sheet for 12 to 15 minutes, or until golden. Remove them from the baking sheet and let them cool on cooling rack.

Note: For variety, instead of preserves, for the filling use 3 ounces (handmade non-vegetable gum) cream cheese, found in specialty stores, mixed with 2 1/2 teaspoons honey.

Serves 15 (15 Hamentaschen)

Opposite page: Photo, 1980. The famous Art Ginsburg, proprietor of Art's Deli in Los Angeles, California. *(Courtesy of Art's Deli)*

Art's Deli

"There is an *Art* to making a sandwich!" Anyone who knows Art Ginsburg and anyone who comes here for the monstrous sandwiches knows that this man knows what he is doing.

In the heart of the San Fernando Valley, north of Los Angeles, sits this old-time Jewish deli. Started when Ventura Boulevard was the main drag and before the famous 101 Ventura Freeway was built, his deli was positioned perfectly. It is close to the movie and television studios, and there is even an executive booth with a hidden phone where many movie and television deals have been made.

Beginning with just three booths and twelve counter stools, the deli has grown and expanded four times since it opened here in 1957. Gold vinyl and Formica dominate the décor with poster-sized photos of deli sandwiches. But no one comes here for the interior decoration. As Art explains, "It's how comfortable you feel when you walk in." Isn't that the true deli experience?

When Art's Deli burned down after the 1994 earthquake, customers catered to their favorite gathering place by bringing food to the deli. Feeding the masses all those years paid off with their loyalty.

Art's Deli serves 1,000 pounds of corned beef and 400 bagels every week. And with turkey becoming the substitute for the cholesterol-laden meats, at least in sunny California, 25,000 pounds of turkey are served each year. With each triple-decker combination sandwich holding one pound of meat, even weight-conscious Californians can't resist. The bean and barley soup is a vegetarian's nirvana, and the creamy rice pudding definitely wins the prize for the most scrumptious rice pudding ever. Art's Deli is a deli extraordinaire!

Menu art, 1994. *(Courtesy of Art's Deli)*

Art's Deli Potato Salad

6 russet potatoes, with skins

3 celery stalks, chopped

1 yellow onion, grated

1 cup mayonnaise

2 tablespoons Dijon mustard

1/2 teaspoon salt

1/2 teaspoon black pepper

In a large pot, cook the potatoes on medium-high heat for 30 to 35 minutes, or until they are tender. Drain and peel the potatoes. For a firm potato salad, cover and refrigerate the boiled potatoes overnight before proceeding. Cut the chilled potatoes into cubes and place them in a large bowl. Add the celery and onion. In a separate bowl, combine the mayonnaise, mustard, salt, and pepper. Pour the mayonnaise mixture over the potatoes and toss them to mix well. Taste to correct the seasonings. If it is too dry, add more mayonnaise. Add more mustard if you wish. Refrigerate, and serve cold.

Serves 6 (8 cups)

Art's Deli Bean and Barley Soup

1 1/2 cups pearl barley

1 cup green split peas

1 cup dried and packaged lentils

1 cup dried and packaged baby lima beans

8 medium tomatoes, finely chopped

4 carrots, peeled and finely diced

1 large yellow onion, finely diced

4 stalks celery, finely diced

1 (16-ounce) can tomato sauce

1 large beef bone or 4 short ribs (omit for a vegetarian version)

Salt and white pepper, to taste

4 quarts water

Put all the ingredients into a large soup pot. Cook them over medium heat for 3 hours, or until the beans are soft. Stir occasionally to make sure the beans do not stick to bottom of the pot. Place the soup pot in an ice water bath (in a sink filled with enough ice water to equal 1/2 of the size of the pot) to quickly bring down the temperature. This will stop the beans from cooking. If the soup is too thick, add water. If it's too thin, add pearl barley to thicken.

Serves 30 to 32

Art's Deli Potato Latkes

3 russet potatoes

1 yellow onion

2 large eggs

Salt and black pepper, to taste

1/2 cup matzo meal

Vegetable oil, for frying

Applesauce, for serving

Sour cream, for serving

Peel the potatoes and onion and grate them into a large bowl. Press them to remove as much water as possible. Beat the eggs separately and add them to the potatoes. Mix them until they are well blended. Add salt and pepper and enough matzo meal to bind the eggs to the potatoes. The mixture should hold its shape in a spoon when tapped against the side of the bowl. Heat the oil on medium heat until bubbles form on the surface, and drop the large spoonfuls of potato mixture into the oil, being careful to keep the latkes from touching each other. Fry in the oil until they are golden brown on both sides. Drain the latkes on paper towels and keep them covered until you are ready to serve them. The latkes are delicious when served with applesauce or sour cream on the side.

Serves 6 to 8 (6 to 8 latkes)

Photo, 1953. Canter's Deli has boasted beautiful baked goods for years. *(Courtesy of Canter's Deli)*

Photo, 1965. Ben Canter with three of his favorite waitresses and a cashier. These ladies were paramount in making the deli run properly and were with Canter's for more than 35 years. *(Courtesy of Canter's Deli)*

Canter's Deli

Any time of the day or night, pastrami sandwiches, with the most heavenly fresh-baked rye bread, are ready and waiting at Canter's Deli, one of California's oldest delis, located in Los Angeles's Miracle Mile District — the heart and soul of the entertainment industry. Not much has changed at Canter's Deli except its size: it has expanded twice in its seventy-plus years, making it — at 14,000 square feet — one of the largest delis in the United States.

It all began in 1924 in Jersey City, New Jersey. After losing a deli in the 1929 stock market crash, Ben Canter and his two brothers moved to California with just $500 in their pockets. Eager to succeed, they opened Canter Brothers Delicatessen in 1931 on Brooklyn Avenue in Boyle Heights, the Jewish center of Los Angeles. When this cultural hotspot shifted, friends Harold Prince and Selma Udko partnered with Ben and his wife, Jenny, to purchase a prime location at 439 North Fairfax Avenue. In 1953 they purchased the old Esquire Theater at 419 North Fairfax and moved Canter's Deli just up the street to a larger location. In those days Ben Canter would sell two hot dogs for 5 cents — one in a bun and one in your hand.

For over fifty years this third-generation family-owned business has served food to locals, tourists, and celebrities alike. With its Art Deco décor and its trademark autumn leaves ceiling, this hangout has hardly changed in this last half century. It is here in the front booth where Lenny Bruce used to sit munching on knockwurst while writing skits. Mel Brooks, Buddy Hackett, Bill Cosby, David Brenner, Rodney Dangerfield, Danny Thomas, Henry Winkler, and Dick Van Dyke frequented Canter's Deli. Marilyn Monroe and Arthur Miller dined here, Jack Benny, Elizabeth Taylor, Cary Grant, Nicolas Cage, John Travolta, even Elvis and the Beatles have sat at Canter's Deli booths. Local and national politicians, Mayors Bradley and Giuliani, governors and senators congregated here to meet and campaign. The list is endless. It's a haven for late-night musicians. The Doors and Frank Zappa ate here, meeting in the Kibbitz Room, a 1965 addition that is also a cocktail lounge. On Tuesday nights, informal star-studded jam sessions took place where the groups would rehearse, schmooze, and kibbitz. Many, including Joni Mitchell, Rick James, and members of the Red Hot Chili Peppers, have come here to hang out, sing, play, and, most importantly, to eat.

Photo, 1953. A newly remodeled Formica interior.
(Courtesy of Canter's Deli)

Photo, 2002. Gary Canter hosting New York Mayor Rudy Giuliani on a visit to the deli.
(Courtesy of Canter's Deli)

You wouldn't think that Los Angeles could have a deli to rival New York's, but for those who know and love deli culture and appreciate all that it evokes, this place is heaven. Voted the "#1 Best Pastrami" by *The Los Angeles Times*, Canter's Deli sandwiches are always served on rye, unless you ask for something else, but don't do that! Made famous for its corned beef and salami sandwich, Canter's Deli boasts of serving the best quality at reasonable prices. The two generations of Canters that are always present have an intense pride in their deli. Alan Canter is there seven days a week. His son, Gary Canter, sister Jackie, and brother Mark are like family to all who enter.

And when you do enter, you are greeted by what may be the most sumptuous bakery counter in America. Cheesecake, babka, sour cream coffee cakes, rugelach, mandelbrot, black and white cookies, tea cookies, strudels, chocolate cakes, carrot cakes, bagels, rye bread, pumpernickel, challah, and more are baked on the premises twice a day. Canter's Deli makes its own pickles and knishes, and it even has an entire refrigerated room filled with nothing but matzo balls, ready and waiting to be coupled with the deli's rich

chicken broth. Everything here is made fresh daily, with no preservatives, and everything unused goes to charity.

Canter's Deli boasts having sold 2 million pounds of lox, 9 million pounds of corned beef, 10 million matzo balls, 20 million bagels, 24 million bowls of chicken soup, and 3 million pounds of potato salad. And to accommodate changing eating habits, it now offers anything from Chinese chicken salad to quesadillas. It even offers an entire Thanksgiving dinner on the menu every day.

Tour buses stop here, and many tourists eat here as well, but the real heart and soul of this deli are the locals who have never moved from the neighborhood and the stars who slip in here incognito for a late night nosh. Canter's Deli is a place of solace, and they come for the old-fashioned Jewish food that reminds them of their past. Open twenty-four hours and only closed on Jewish holidays, you can come here anytime for a delicious taste of yesterday.

Canter's Deli Marble Cake

3 cups sugar

1 tablespoon salt

3/4 teaspoon baking powder

2 tablespoons nonfat dry milk powder

2 1/2 cups cake flour

6 eggs

1 1/4 cup shortening

1 cup water

1/4 cup chocolate syrup

Preheat the oven to 350 degrees. Grease 2 loaf pans.

Using an electric mixer on medium speed, mix the sugar, salt, baking powder, milk powder, cake flour, eggs, and shortening. Add the water and mix for an additional 2 minutes on medium. Drizzle the chocolate syrup over the batter, then cut through the batter with a knife several times to give a marbled appearance. Bake for 35 to 40 minutes, until it is golden.

Serves 8 (2 loaves)

Canter's Deli Brisket of Beef

1 cup ketchup

1 cup mustard

1/2 cup granulated garlic

1 teaspoon black pepper

1 (12-pound) brisket

5 carrots, peeled and sliced lengthwise

5 celery stalks

5 russet potatoes, peeled and quartered

5 yellow onions, chopped

5 garlic cloves, peeled

Preheat the oven to 350 degrees.

Mix together the ketchup, mustard, granulated garlic, and black pepper in a medium bowl, and rub into the beef. Place the beef in a roasting pan, add 1/3 of the vegetables to the pan, and fill it with 2 cups of water. Cover the pan with aluminum foil. Roast in the oven for 3 1/2 hours, or until the meat is browned and fork tender. About 1 hour before the brisket is done, add the potatoes and the remaining vegetables to the pan. For extra flavor, add the garlic. Cover again with the foil and continue roasting until it is done. Let the brisket rest for ten minutes so the juices do not run out, then slice it against the grain.

Serves 8 to 10

Canter's Deli Coleslaw

4 cups sugar

4 cups sour cream

4 cups mayonnaise

1/2 cup freshly-squeezed lemon juice

1/2 cup white vinegar

1/4 cup white horseradish

Salt and pepper, to taste

5 whole white or purple cabbages, shredded

Mix the first seven ingredients in a large bowl. Mix in the cabbage. Season with salt and pepper to taste. Chill at least 1 hour. (The coleslaw can be made 1 day ahead and should be refrigerated.)

Serves 15 to 20

Canter's Deli Homemade Pickles

1/2 gallon water

1/2 cup salt

10 cloves garlic, peeled and chopped

1/2 cup pickling spices

1/2 cup chopped fresh dill

1/2 teaspoon chili pepper flakes

7 bay leaves

15 small, firm cucumbers

Mix together all the ingredients except the cucumbers in a 1-gallon container. Add the cucumbers. Store at room temperature for seven days. Do not cover; they need air to pickle correctly. Store in the refrigerator for up to 1 month.

Makes 15

Canter's Deli Chocolate Chip Rugelach

2 pounds cream cheese, at room temperature

2 pounds (8 sticks) butter, at room temperature

2 pounds enriched flour

1/2 pound sugar

3 pounds chocolate chips

1 pound sour cream

Cream the cream cheese and butter in a mixer on medium speed until they are blended. Add the flour and sugar to the cream cheese mixture and continue beating until all the ingredients are combined. Add the chips and mix until they are evenly distributed throughout the dough. Turn out the dough onto a large cookie sheet and flatten with your hands. Place the cookie sheet in the refrigerator to rest for 5 hours.

Preheat the oven to 350 degrees.

Remove the dough from the refrigerator, and place it on a lightly floured work surface. Roll it out to a 1/2-inch thickness. Spread a thin layer of sour cream on the dough and roll it in a jelly-roll fashion. Slice the dough into 1-inch lengths, place the pieces evenly on a greased baking sheet, and bake for 30 to 40 minutes until they are golden. Repeat with the remaining dough until it is baked. Rugelach freezes beautifully for 3 to 4 months.

Serves 8 to 10 (35 rugelach)

Photo, 1960. Pierre Salinger meeting with the Canter's Deli heads of state, Albert Canter, Alan Canter, and Jack Baker. *(Courtesy of Canter's Deli)*

Canter's Deli Cheese Blintzes

Crêpes:

3 large eggs

1/4 cup water

1/4 cup milk

1/2 teaspoon baking powder

1/2 cup all-purpose flour

1 1/2 teaspoons sugar

1/2 tablespoon unsalted butter,
   plus more for frying

Cheese filling:

2 pounds farmer cheese

1 egg, beaten

1/3 cup sugar

1 teaspoon pure vanilla extract

Garnish:

Sour cream

Blueberry or strawberry preserves

Combine the crêpe ingredients in a blender and let them stand 30 minutes.

In an 8-inch nonstick skillet, melt 1/2 a tablespoon of butter over moderately high heat. Pour in enough batter to just coat the bottom of the skillet, swirling, and cook it undisturbed until the top is set and the bottom is golden. (Do not turn it over.) Transfer the crêpe to paper towels in one layer, with the golden side down. Make more crêpes with the remaining batter. Use more butter as needed.

Mix all the cheese filling ingredients together in a large bowl. With a large spoon, place 3 tablespoons of filling in the center of each crêpe; fold the opposite sides of the crêpe over the filling until the sides barely touch. Fold in the ends to completely enclose the filling, forming packets. Heat butter in a frying pan on medium heat, and place 6 blintzes in the pan. Cook on both sides until they are golden. Repeat with the remaining blintzes. Serve them warm with sour cream and/or preserves on the side.

Serves 6 (12 blintzes)

Mural, modern. *(Courtesy of D. Z. Akins Deli)*

D. Z. Akin's Deli

San Diego was in great need of a delicatessen, and D. Z. Akin's Deli arrived to fill the bill. When Debbie and her Israeli-born husband, Zvika Akin, ventured to San Diego from Los Angeles in 1980, they saw the need for a Jewish deli similar to the ones they had grown up with. With absolutely no experience and just in their mid-20s, the two did not generate visions of yesteryear's deli owner, but perhaps this is a new era of the deli experience.

Debbie and Zvika's determination was obvious. They opened a deli in the most unlikely of places — a strip shopping center in a less-than-accessible spot right off the freeway. Local celebrities and the occasional politician dine there, fueled by the need and desire for a corned beef sandwich and searching for a sense of community that D. Z. Akin's Deli hopes to offer.

There is already a second generation involved, as their son, Neil, has taken over the helm. Like so many delis of the past, the second generation is now in place.

D. Z. Akin's Deli utilizes the ubiquitous formula so important for a delicatessen — hard work, loyal employees, comforting food, and a gathering place for lonely East Coasters. As they say, build it and they will come!

D.Z. Akin's restaurant and delicatessen

6930 Alvarado Road, San Diego, California 92120

Call For Take-Out Orders
And Party Platters
(714) 265-0218

Full Delicatessen Take-Out
Cold-Cuts, Smoked-Fish, Cheeses,
and Home-Made Salads By the Pound.

Menu. 1985. *(Courtesy of D. Z. Akin's Deli)*

D. Z. Akin's Deli Florentine Cookies

1 cup (2 sticks) butter or margarine

1 cup whipping cream

2 cups sugar

1/4 cup glucose syrup (available at
any cake supplier)

1/4 cup bread flour

3 cups sliced almonds

Chocolate, for coating (optional)

Place the butter or margarine, whipping cream, sugar, and glucose in a double boiler and heat over medium heat until the sugar is dissolved. Combine the flour with the almonds in a bowl and add them to the liquid in the boiler. Let the mixture cool for about 30 minutes. Meanwhile, preheat the oven to 340 degrees and line 2 baking sheets with parchment paper. Place marble-size spoonfuls of the cookie batter 3 inches apart on the prepared baking sheets. You should have 16 florentines on each pan. Bake the cookies for 8 to 10 minutes, or until they are flat. Remove them from the oven and cool them on a rack. When the cookies are cool, coat them in chocolate if you wish.

Makes 32

D. Z. Akin's Deli Reuben Sandwich

1 teaspoon butter

2 slices rye bread

2 slices (2 ounces) Swiss cheese

1⁄2 cup sauerkraut

6 slices (6 ounces) corned beef or pastrami

Spread the butter on 1 side of each piece of bread, and place them on a heated grill. (Alternatively, heat a frying pan over medium heat, put 1 teaspoon of butter in the pan, and place the sandwich in the pan for 5 minutes.) Put 1 slice of cheese on each piece of bread while they are still on the grill. Heat the sauerkraut in a separate pan, then put it on top of one bread slice. Add the meat and top with the second slice of bread. Turn the sandwich over and cook for 5 minutes. Cut in half and serve immediately.

Serves 1 (1 large sandwich)

Above: Photo, 2001. A pastrami, turkey, and corned beef on rye with a Dr. Brown's soda. A quintessential deli meal! *(Courtesy of D. Z. Akin's Deli)*

D. Z. Akin's Deli Potato Soup

2 cups (4 sticks) butter

2 sweet Vidalia onions

1/2 cup all-purpose flour

10 russet potatoes, quartered

2 carrots, peeled and sliced

Salt and pepper, to taste

1 teaspoon dried dill (optional)

4 quarts water or chicken broth

Melt the butter in a large soup pot, add the onions, and let them sauté on medium heat until they are light brown. Add the flour and stir it to make a roux. Add the potatoes, carrots, salt, pepper, dill, and water. Bring them to a boil, then lower the heat and simmer for 1 1/2 hours until the potatoes are soft.

Serves 10

Photo, 2004. Factor's Famous Deli interior, complete with deli counter. *(Courtesy of Factor's Famous Deli)*

Photo, 2003. *(Courtesy of Factor's Famous Deli)*

Factor's Famous Deli

"Your home away from home" is the mantra of the Markowitz family, which has been at the helm of Factor's Famous Deli since 1969. The business

was opened in 1948 by Abe and Esther Factor and is still at the original location on Pico Boulevard in Los Angeles, California. Being close to the movie and television studios, there is a constant stream of people coming in and catering orders going out.

Before immigrating to America from Prague before WWII, Herman and Lili Markowitz owned a landmark restaurant that was known throughout Europe. As Holocaust survivors, they came to America with a dream of a better life. Having lost everything in their homeland, they sought to build a new life. But the dream of

Herman Markowitz was short-lived, as he lived for only five years while owning and operating Factor's Famous Deli. Lili was left with five children and the task of running the restaurant.

The biggest change in the deli's business is that 80 percent of its clientele uses the deli as a sole source of food for the holidays. To meet the demand, Factor's opened a large catering facility separate from its vast deli. Now its yummy smoked fish brunches and sweet and sour cabbage can be picked up and taken home anytime of the day or night.

True to tradition, the Factor's Famous Deli waitstaff has been with the deli for many years. One beloved waitress just retired at the age of ninety-six! With their staff, the Markowitz daughters, Debbie and Susie, continue the Factor's Famous Deli legacy, committed to keeping the tradition alive.

Above: Menu, 2004. *(Courtesy of Factor's Famous Deli)*

Opposite page: Postcard, 2003. *(Courtesy of Marlene Zimmerman)*

Factor's Famous Deli Turkey Loaf

1/2 yellow onion, chopped

1 carrot, peeled and chopped

1 green bell pepper, peeled, de-ribbed, and chopped

2 pounds ground turkey

2 eggs, beaten

2 teaspoons Worcestershire sauce

2 cloves garlic

1/4 teaspoon ground cumin

1/4 teaspoon oregano

1/4 teaspoon white pepper

Preheat the oven to 325 degrees.

Put the onions, carrots, and bell pepper in the bowl of a food processor fitted with the metal blade, and pulse to grind. Place the turkey in a large bowl and add the ground vegetable mix. Add the eggs, Worcestershire sauce, garlic, cumin, oregano, and white pepper. Mix well, and place the mixture in a loaf pan. Cook for 30 minutes, or until it is brown. The turkey loaf can be served hot or cold.

Serves 6

Factor's Famous Deli Lentil Soup

3 cups lentils

3 tablespoons olive oil

1 carrot, peeled and chopped

1/2 white onion, peeled and chopped

1/2 celery stalk, peeled and chopped

3 cloves garlic, peeled and chopped

1 tablespoon chicken bouillon

1/4 teaspoon white pepper

1 bay leaf

1 whole clove

8 cups water

Boil the lentils until they are soft, about 30 minutes. Sauté the vegetables in olive oil. Add the vegetable mix, garlic, chicken bouillon, white pepper, bay leaf, clove, and water to the lentils. Bring the soup to a boil. Reduce the heat to low and simmer for 1 1/2 hours, or until the lentils and vegetables are soft.

Serves 10 to 15

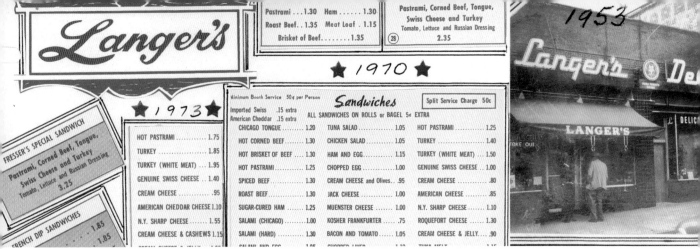

Langer's Deli

Why pastrami? Why indeed! This venerable Los Angeles deli has declared pastrami as its claim to fame, and it's obvious why.

Langer's Deli opened its doors on June 17, 1947, on Alvarado Street in Los Angeles and has remained there ever since. Starting with only three windows fronting the street, it expanded, taking over a bank and other spaces to eventually dominate the corner of Alvarado and Seventh. Even with the changing neighborhood and concerns about safety, it has remained in the same location. Langer's now closes at four in the afternoon and does not open on Sunday, which in the deli business is notoriously one of the busiest days, but it continues to attract loyal patrons during the week. The subway opening in Los Angeles in the mid-1990s was a boon to business in that area. Named "The Pastrami Express," the metro red liner would carry hungry diners from their offices in downtown Los Angeles right to Langer's Deli's doorstep.

The late Al Langer had a long history in the deli business. He began at eleven years old, working in a deli in Newark, New Jersey, and it was there that he learned his trade and developed his unique method for preparing pastrami. After arriving in Los Angeles in 1937, he met the woman he married; she was working as a waitress at the time. They were married for more than sixty years.

Keeping with the tradition of the old-time delis, Norm Langer, the second generation, now runs the restaurant, most assuredly with his father's blessing.

"Now, as for the pastrami, it could either be great or it could taste like smoked rubber bands," explains Norm Langer. "It's all in the preparation, the cut of meat, and the way it is sliced — that's what determines its flavor."

Norm is the only deli man known to divulge his secret to pastrami, and since he is a "pastrami maven," we are grateful he has shared his process for this perfect tender, chewy, peppery, sour, and smoky cut of beef.

Langer's Deli Pastrami-Making Tips

First you need to know that after the navel cut of beef is steamed it shrinks 25 percent, making it the reason for the more costly price. Figure that with an 1,800-pound steer, you get two pounds of navel meat. The square cut is then sugar-cured, seasoned with the appropriate spices, and after it is steamed and the fat and sinew removed, you are left with 1 1/2 pounds of edible meat.

The custom-made steamer at Langer's has a constant live steam that steams the rock-hard meat for 3 hours (as opposed to the more common 2 to 2 1/2 hours) at an internal temperature of 210 degrees to break down the tissues. This is key! Then it is cut only by hand, and only across the grain.

(As they say at Langer's, they cater to the piece of meat!)

Langer's Deli Mushroom Barley Soup

This is an excellent soup for a large party or gathering, and Mr. Langer insists that reducing the recipe would negatively affect the soup's wonderful flavors.

4 gallons water
5 pounds chicken giblets
6 cups uncooked barley
2 (16-ounce) cans mushrooms
3/4 pint chicken soup base
3 medium carrots, peeled and sliced
1/2 teaspoon salt
Pinch of white pepper

Place the chicken giblets in a large soup pot filled with water and bring it to a boil. Lower the heat and simmer for 2 hours. Add the remaining ingredients and continue to boil for 1 1/2 hours more.

Serves 60 (16 quarts)

Langer's Deli Cabbage Soup

**This is another great soup for a crowd. Mr. Langer
stands by the flavor of his soups when made in
bulk. Reducing recipes is out of the question!**

- 4 gallons chicken broth, plus more as
  needed for thinning
- 2 cups (16-ounce) canned tomato purée
- 6 pounds whole stewed tomatoes
- 3 carrots, grated
- 10 heads green cabbage
- 1/4 cup citric acid or sour salt (found in the
  spice section of specialty markets)
- 1 tablespoon salt
- 1 tablespoon chicken-flavored soup base
- 1 tablespoon sugar
- 1 pint sauerkraut
- 5 russet potatoes, boiled and cubed

**Bring the chicken broth to a boil. Add all the
ingredients except the potatoes to the chicken
broth and let them boil for 1 hour, or until the
cabbage is soft. Add the potatoes and simmer for
an additional hour. If the broth is thickening more
than desired, add more chicken broth to thin it.
Cook for 1 1/2 hours.**

Serves 60 (16 quarts)

Top: Photo, 1960. Al and Norm Langer behind
the counter of their famous Los Angeles Deli.
(Courtesy of Langer's Deli)

Opposite page and above: Menu, 2003.
(Courtesy of Langer's Deli)

Breakfast at *Langer's*

Eggs & Omelettes

BACON or LINK SAUSAGE and 3 EGGS	7.95
HAM and 3 EGGS	7.95
HAMBURGER PATTY and 3 EGGS	7.95
SALAMI and 3 EGGS Pancake Style	7.95
SCRAMBLED GROUND BEEF, EGGS & ONIONS	7.95
SCRAMBLED LOX, EGGS & ONIONS	10.50
SCRAMBLED EGGS - LOX on the Side	11.50
CORNED BEEF or PASTRAMI and 3 EGGS Pancake Style	8.95
CORNED BEEF HASH and 3 EGGS	7.95
FRIED KIPPERS Onions and Potatoes	8.95
FRIED KIPPERS, ONIONS and 3 EGGS	9.95
MATZO BREI Pancake or Scrambled	6.95

THREE EGGS . . . . .4.65   with Onions 4.90
TWO EGGS . . . . .4.40   with Onions 4.65
ONE EGG . . . . .4.25   with Onions 4.50

EGG WHITES or BEATERS $1.00 EXTRA

> STEAK and 3 EGGS 11.50
> HAM STEAK and 3 EGGS 10.75

70	WESTERN OMELETTE Assorted Deli Meats	8.95
71	AMERICAN CHEESE OMELETTE	7.95
72	SPANISH OMELETTE	8.25
73	MUSHROOM OMELETTE	8.25
74	CHICKEN LIVER OMELETTE	8.95
75	ALVARADO OMELETTE Lean Ground Beef, Spinach and Onions	8.95
76	CHILI & CHEESE OMELETTE	8.95
77	SPINACH OMELETTE	8.25
78	ORTEGA CHILE OMELETTE Chile Peppers, Onions, Tomato & Cheese	8.95
79	HAM OMELETTE . . . . .8.50 with Cheese	8.95
82	DENVER OMELETTE	8.95

> **PLATTER of WHITEFISH, LOX & CREAM CHEESE 25.00**
> Served with Tomatoes, Olives, Onions & Three Bagels (Serves Two)

LOX, CREAM CHEESE and SWISS CHEESE PLATE 18.95
LOX & CREAM CHEESE SANDWICH on Bread, Bagel or Roll 11.50

HOT CEREALS - 3.95   COLD CEREALS - 3.25

Appetizers

Includes Bread and Butter

WHITEFISH or LOX & CREAM CHEESE	12.50
PICKLED HERRING	5.75
CANNED TUNA	8.95

Fruits & Juices

*Fresh Fruit In Season

GRAPEFRUIT JUICE	1.75 & 2.25
ORANGE JUICE	1.75 & 2.25
APPLE JUICE	1.75 & 2.25
APPLE SAUCE	2.25
SLICED PEACHES	2.60

Side Orders

Cream Cheese	1.75
Home Fries	2.75
Bread or Roll and Butter	1.95
English Muffin	1.95
Danish Roll	
Blueberry and Bran Muffins	
Link Sausage	3.95
Bacon	3.95
Ham	4.45
Hamburger Patty	4.25
Corned Beef Hash	5.25
One Egg	2.35
Two Eggs	2.85

Fountain Treats

EGG CREAM	1.95
MALTS or SHAKES	3.25
SODAS, Chocolate/Strawberry	3.25
ROOT BEER FLOAT	3.25
CHOCOLATE PHOSPHATE	1.95
CHOCOLATE MILK	2.25
STRAWBERRY SUNDAE	3.75
CHOCOLATE SUNDAE	3.75

EL PASO'S FINEST

Mac's

DELICATESSEN

1 MAC'S SPECIAL
Tongue-Corned Beef & Salami
Potato Salad or Slaw
Kosher Dill Pickle
2.00
2 DECKER

2 RITA'S SPECIAL
Pastrami-Tongue & Swiss Cheese
Potato Salad or Slaw
Kosher Dill Pickle
2.00
2 DECKER

3 LENNY'S SPECIAL
Corned Beef-Chopped Liver & Swiss Cheese
Potato Salad or Slaw
Kosher Dill Pickle
2.00
2 DECKER

SANDWICHES

COLD PEPPER BEEF	1.35
HOT CORNED BEEF	1.35
KING SIZE	2.25
HOT PASTRAMI	1.35
KING SIZE	2.25
TONGUE	1.35
KING SIZE	2.25
HAM ON RYE	1.35
SALAMI	1.25
HARD SALAMI	1.50
BOLOGNA	1.25
CHOPPED LIVER	1.35
LIVERWURST	1.25
DOMESTIC SWISS	1.10
IMPORTED SWISS	1.35
MUENSTER CHEESE	1.10
NEW YORK SHARP	1.35
CREAM CHEESE ON RYE	1.00
CREAM CHEESE ON BAGEL	1.00
LOX & CREAM CHEESE ON RYE	1.75
LOX & CREAM CHEESE ON BAGEL	1.75
ROAST BEEF on French or Kaiser Roll	1.35
KOSHER FRANK	.90
KNOCKWURST	1.25

All Sandwiches served with Potato Salad or Cole Slaw & Pickle
With Swiss Cheese .15 Extra   With Imported Cheese .25 Extra

GRILLED REUBEN SANDWICH 1.75
Corned Beef & Swiss Cheese, Sauerkraut, Potato Salad or Slaw, Kosher Dill Pickle

SKINLESS AND BONELESS OR NORWEGIAN SARDINE SANDWICH 1.50
Lettuce, Tomato, Onion, Potato Salad or Cole Slaw & Pickle

BEVERAGES

COFFEE (1 FILL)	.20
ICED TEA (1 FILL)	.20
HOT TEA	.20
SOFT DRINKS	.25
MILK	.20
BUTTERMILK	.20
SANKA	.25
EASTERN BEERS	.60

RELISHES & SIDE ORDERS

BUTTERED TOAST	.25	BAGEL	.25
FRENCH FRIES	.50	KAISER ROLL	.25
POTATO SALAD	.50	FRENCH ROLL	.25
COLE SLAW	.50	DOMESTIC SWISS	.75
DILL PICKLES	.35	IMPORTED SWISS	1.00
BAKED BEANS	.50		
GRECIAN OLIVES	.65		
CREAM CHEESE	.65		
SOUR CREAM	.65		

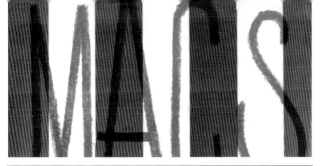

Mac's Delicatessen
Russian Cabbage Borscht

3 yellow onions, chopped

2 cloves garlic, minced

3 tablespoons butter

3 pounds center-cut chuck

All-purpose flour

2 (15-ounce) cans tomato purée

1 (6-ounce) can tomato paste

3/4 cup brown sugar

Juice of 3 lemons

1 head cabbage

2 bay leaves

Salt and pepper to taste

Brown onions and half the minced garlic in butter in covered heavy Dutch oven. Cut chuck into bite-sized pieces, dust with flour. Place in the pot with the onion and garlic. Allow to brown lightly uncovered, then cover and allow the gravy to collect by simmering on low for about 1 1/2 hours.

Add tomato purée and tomato paste to the stockpot. Make a sweet and sour sauce by adding the brown sugar, lemon juice of the lemons, and bay leaves Cook slowly over low heat 20 minutes. Add cabbage and cook on low heat for 3 1/2 hours covered. Just before serving, mash together the remaining minced garlic and the salt and pepper. Add enough water to make a paste. Cook for an additional 1/2 hour. If the soup is too thick, add water.

Serves 10

Opposite page and above: Menu, 1960s. *(Courtesy of Rita Silverman)*

Mac's Delicatessen

In west Texas, where Mexican food is king, this much-loved deli served delicious, authentic deli foods for twenty-six years. Maybe it survived in this unlikely place because the owner, Mac Fagelman, a decorated WWII veteran with a Silver Star, knew how to appeal to the servicemen at Fort Bliss, the army base headquartered in El Paso, Texas. Or maybe it was because the food was just so good.

How did Mac's Delicatessen make its debut in west Texas, of all places? Mac, as he was called, was escaping the Detroit weather and was on his way to live in Arizona. He and his wife, Grace, stopped off in El Paso, and decided to remain there and open a small grocery store. Like many other delis that opened in the 1940s, Mac's soon grew into a full-service deli, serving corned beef sandwiches as good as anything you could have found in New York City.

Armed with Mac's experience as a meat cutter and possessing old family recipes, the couple served the town well. Walking into Mac's brought many servicemen the comfort that they missed from home. In those days, in towns like El Paso, everybody knew everybody. Here, when you walked in the door, Mac would always yell out your name. It was just so incongruous for this little bit of New York to be nestled in the middle of the Southwest, but for the residents of this west Texas town, it was a place of community never to be seen again. When delis like this close, it is more than sad. It is a great loss to the landscape of the towns and cities they inhabited.

Photo, 1947. Nate 'n Al's Beverly Boulevard location. *(Courtesy of Nate 'n Al's Delicatessen)*

Photo, circa 1945. A classic deli counter photo, featuring Nate 'n Al's founder, Al Mendelson, and counterman Abe. *(Courtesy of Nate 'n Al's Delicatessen)*

Nate 'n Al's Delicatessen

On any given day, if celebrities are what you seek, just take a booth at the famed Nate 'n Al's Delicatessen in Beverly Hills. Order a bagel with lox, cream cheese, and sliced onion, and watch the parade of movie and television stars, politicians, and local dignitaries dining, unbothered by adoring fans. Larry King, Robert Wagner, Neil Diamond, John Voigt, and Kareem Abdul Jabbar are just some who come often to meet old friends and be a part of the history that prevails in this old-time deli environment. Nate 'n Al's Delicatessen is not as much a tourist mecca as some of the delis in New York City might be; it is an established, well-known deli, catering to local patrons, and featuring great service and sumptuous deli food.

It all began in 1923, when Russian-born Al Mendelson immigrated from Toronto, Canada, to Detroit. He met Nate Reimer while working in another well-known but now shuttered deli, Boesky's. There they formed their partnership and opened a small delicatessen on North Beverly Drive in Los Angeles in 1945. The deli would become a legend in the deli world. After Nate passed away in the late 1940s, Al and his wife, Tessie, who ran the cash register for more than thirty years, continued to operate the restaurant under the same name. The deli got a little bit larger in the 1950s, but the look never changed. Its success was enough to prove that the deli was perfect just the way it was.

As it is with all of the old-time delis, the staff is also family. Many of the loyal and friendly waitresses have been there for twenty to thirty years. Kaye Coleman, a longtime waitress at Nate 'n Al's, was interviewed on *The Larry King Show*. Jay Kornblum, the manager and resident everyman, doesn't think of his commitment as a job; it's his life.

Al Mendelson's charitable contributions to many organizations and charities made him a celebrity in his own right, and when movie studios wanted to buy into the famed deli, he just wanted to keep it in the family — the Mendelson family. Never have the Mendelson brothers, Mark and David (third-generation owners and operators), allowed any of their recipes to be published, so when making this creamy whitefish salad or this garlicky corned beef hash, know that you are in a select group that can only dream of experiencing this exclusive trade secret.

TV ad still, 2005. Nate 'n Al's Deli was featured in a Carl's Jr. TV ad campaign to launch the new Pastrami Burger™. *(Courtesy of Carl's Jr.)*

Nate 'n Al's Delicatessen Whitefish Salad

8 pounds whitefish trimmings

2 medium onions, coarsely chopped

1/2 cup mayonnaise

8 celery stalks, chopped

Remove the bones from the whitefish. Place the fish in a large bowl and add the chopped onions. Pulse in the bowl of a food processor fitted with a steel blade until the mixture is smooth. Add the mayonnaise and celery. Chill the salad for thirty minutes and serve cold.

Serves 6 to 8

Nate 'n Al's Delicatessen Corned Beef Hash

8 pounds corned beef ends

4 large russet potatoes, steamed, peeled, and cut into cubes

8 eggs, beaten

1 teaspoon salt

1 1/2 teaspoons garlic powder

1 teaspoon white pepper

In the bowl of a food processor fitted with the steel blade, pulse the corned beef until it is coarsely chopped. Do the same procedure with the potatoes. Then put the potatoes in a large bowl and mix in the eggs, salt, garlic powder, and white pepper; add the corned beef. Cook the mixture over medium heat in a large skillet, using a spatula to press it into the bottom of the skillet, for 15 minutes, or until it is browned on one side. Turn the mixture, in sections if necessary, and continue cooking until it is browned, about 10 minutes. Serve the hash immediately.

Serves 10 to 12

Menu art, circa 1980.
(Courtesy of Nate 'n Al's Delicatessen)

Rose's Deli

Portland, Oregon, has a rich history, and Rose's Deli has played a big part in that. Over fifty years ago, Rose Naftalin, a widow from Toledo, Ohio, moved to Portland and opened a small deli on NW 23rd Avenue. She had owned and operated a small bakery before moving, and was known for her baking skills.

Rose was dedicated. She slept on flour sacks in the back of the store so that by 3:00 a.m. she would be up and ready to bake. This little deli began in 1956, but it was not until Rose retired in 1967 that she realized her dream of establishing a traditional "New York style" deli had come true. Grandma Rose, as she was affectionately called, was first and foremost a baker and a dessert cookbook author, and the delectable desserts that grace the bakery counter of Rose's today are a testament to her unique skills.

Rose's closed in 1980 but was purchased in 1992 by Richard Werth, a former New Yorker who made it his mission to restore Rose's to its past prominence. A new location for Rose's Deli and bakery opened near its original site on NW 23rd Avenue, and

though the red-flocked wallpaper is long gone, the enormous pastry counter is still there as you enter.

Jeff Jetton was brought in as a partner in 1998, and now he and Richard are seeing to it that this beloved landmark and its chain of three other locations continue to grow, prosper, and feed the people of Portland and Vancouver, Washington. The deli is still known for its five different versions of the Reuben sandwich (including the extremely popular turkey Reuben), but it's the enormous and mouthwatering desserts that keep customers coming back to remember the Rose's Deli of yesteryear.

Rose's Deli Chicken Broth

5 carrots, peeled and chopped

3 large yellow onions, peeled and quartered

4 stalks celery, chopped

3 bay leaves

1 tablespoon black peppercorns

3 tablespoons fresh thyme, chopped

8 garlic cloves, peeled and crushed

2 tablespoons fresh chopped dill

3 tablespoons kosher salt

2 (2 1/2- to 3-pound) whole chickens, with livers removed and rinsed with water

Place all of the ingredients in a large stockpot and cover them with cold water. Bring the pot to a simmer over medium-high heat and skim off any foam that rises during cooking. Do not let the broth come to a rolling boil. Simmer for 2 hours. Remove the chickens and use the chicken meat for soup or chicken salad. Strain the broth through a fine-mesh strainer. The broth will keep in the refrigerator for up to one week, or in the freezer for up to 6 months.

Serves 8 to 10

Rose's Deli Egg Custard

8 egg yolks

1/2 cup plus 1 tablespoon sugar

1 teaspoon grated lemon zest

1/2 cup Marsala wine

Ground cinnamon, to taste

Grated fresh nutmeg, to taste

In the top of a double boiler, combine the egg yolks, sugar, and lemon zest. Beat them together with a rotary beater over boiling water while slowly adding the Marsala wine. Do not boil. Scrape the sides of the pan, and when thickened, spoon the mixture into glass dessert dishes. Sprinkle the tops with cinnamon and nutmeg. Serve warm or cold.

Serves 6

Rose's Deli Chopped Chicken Liver

5 tablespoons olive oil

5 pounds chicken livers, drained and patted dry

3 cups red wine

1 large yellow onion, finely chopped

15 cloves garlic, finely chopped

1 cup (2 sticks) butter, cut into pieces

11 hard-boiled eggs, peeled and chilled

1 1/2 cups mayonnaise

1 tablespoon black pepper

2 tablespoons kosher salt

In a large skillet, heat 3 tablespoons of the olive oil. Add the chicken livers and cook them until they are firm. Pour half of the red wine into the hot pan with the livers to deglaze. Cook over medium heat for 20 minutes, or until it is reduced by half. Transfer the liver mixture to a large bowl.

Add the remaining 2 tablespoons of olive oil to the hot pan used for the liver and add the onions. Cook the onions until they are soft, about 10 minutes. Add the garlic and cook for 3 minutes longer. Add the remaining red wine and cook to reduce the liquid by half, about 15 minutes.

Place the liver mixture and the reduced wine mixture in a large bowl. Add the butter and stir gently until the butter is melted. Pour the mixture onto a baking sheet and let it cool. Place half of the liver mixture and half of the eggs into the bowl of a food processor fitted with the metal blade and run until the mixture is smooth. Coarsely chop the eggs and fold them into the chicken liver mixture. Coarsely chop the remaining half of the liver mixture and combine both liver mixtures. Fold in the mayonnaise, salt and pepper, cover with foil or a glass cover, and refrigerate overnight. Serve cold.

Serves 10

Rose's Deli Nocciollette
(Hazelnut Biscuits)

1/2 cup shelled hazelnuts (filberts)

1/2 cup (1 stick) butter

1/3 cup sugar

1 1/2 tablespoons honey

1 cup all-purpose flour

Confectioners' sugar, for dusting

Preheat the oven to 350 degrees. Grease 2 cookie sheets.

Spread the hazelnuts on a baking sheet and put them in the oven for 8 to 10 minutes, until they are lightly toasted. Remove the baking sheets from the oven, and rub the hazelnuts in a kitchen towel to remove the brown skins. Lightly grind the nuts in a food processor. Cream the butter, sugar, and honey together in an electric mixer on medium speed, until the mixture is light and fluffy, then stir in the flour and nuts, mixing to make a smooth dough. With lightly floured hands, pinch off pieces of dough the size of walnuts and shape them into ovals. Arrange the biscuits on baking sheets, about 1 inch apart. Bake them for about 15 minutes, or until they are firm. Cool the biscuits slightly on cooling racks and roll them in confectioners' sugar.

Makes about 2 dozen

Rose's Deli Matzo Balls

12 large eggs, at room temperature

2 tablespoons chopped fresh parsley

1 tablespoon kosher salt

1 teaspoon black pepper

1 3/4 cups soda water, at room temperature

5 tablespoons melted schmaltz
   (chicken fat) or melted butter

3 1/2 cups matzo meal

Break the eggs into a large bowl and add the parsley, salt, and pepper. Whisk the mixture until it is thoroughly blended. Add the soda water, schmaltz, and matzo meal and stir with a wooden spoon just until it is completely incorporated; do not overmix. Let the mixture stand for 20 to 30 minutes at room temperature.

Using a 3-ounce scoop, gently portion out the balls onto a lightly oiled baking sheet. With wet hands (to keep the dough from sticking to you), gently roll the balls until they are smooth. Do not compact the mixture or the matzo balls will turn out tough. Drop the balls into a large stockpot of salted, boiling water and cook for 20 to 25 minutes, stirring every 5 minutes. To test for doneness, insert a toothpick into the balls. It should come out easily, without lifting the ball. Place the balls in hot Rose's Deli Chicken Broth (see page 165) and serve.

Makes 56

Rose's Deli Chicken with Egg and Lemon Sauce

1 (2-pound) whole chicken

1 small yellow onion, sliced

1 small carrot, peeled and sliced

1 small stalk celery, sliced

1 bay leaf

4 peppercorns

1 teaspoon salt, plus more to taste

Freshly ground black pepper

2 tablespoons vegetable oil

2 tablespoons butter

1/4 cup all-purpose flour

2 egg yolks

2 tablespoons chopped fresh parsley, for garnish

Juice and zest of 1 large lemon

Remove the giblets from the chicken and set them aside. Wash the chicken, then quarter, removing the backbone. Put the giblets and backbone into a large saucepan and add the onion, carrot, celery, bay leaf, peppercorns, and 1 teaspoon salt. Cover with cold water, bring to a boil, then cover, reduce heat, and simmer gently over low heat for 30 minutes.

Strain and reserve 1 1/2 cups of the stock. Dry the pieces of chicken with paper towels and season with salt and pepper. Heat the oil and butter together in a wide skillet over low heat, and fry the chicken pieces gently, for 15 minutes, turning frequently until they are golden brown on all sides. Remove the chicken pieces and transfer them to a plate. Sprinkle flour into the pan, stir, and cook for 1 minute. Then gradually stir in the reserved stock. Bring the stock mixture to a boil, stirring constantly. Return the chicken to the pan, cover tightly, and simmer over low heat for 30 to 40 minutes.

Remove the chicken and arrange it on a large serving dish. Put the egg yolks and lemon juice in a small bowl. Add 2 tablespoons of the chicken sauce, and beat lightly. Stir this mixture into the chicken sauce, and heat without boiling. Cook until the sauce is lightly thickened, about 10 minutes. Pour the sauce over the chicken, and garnish with parsley and strips of lemon zest. Serve immediately.

Serves 4

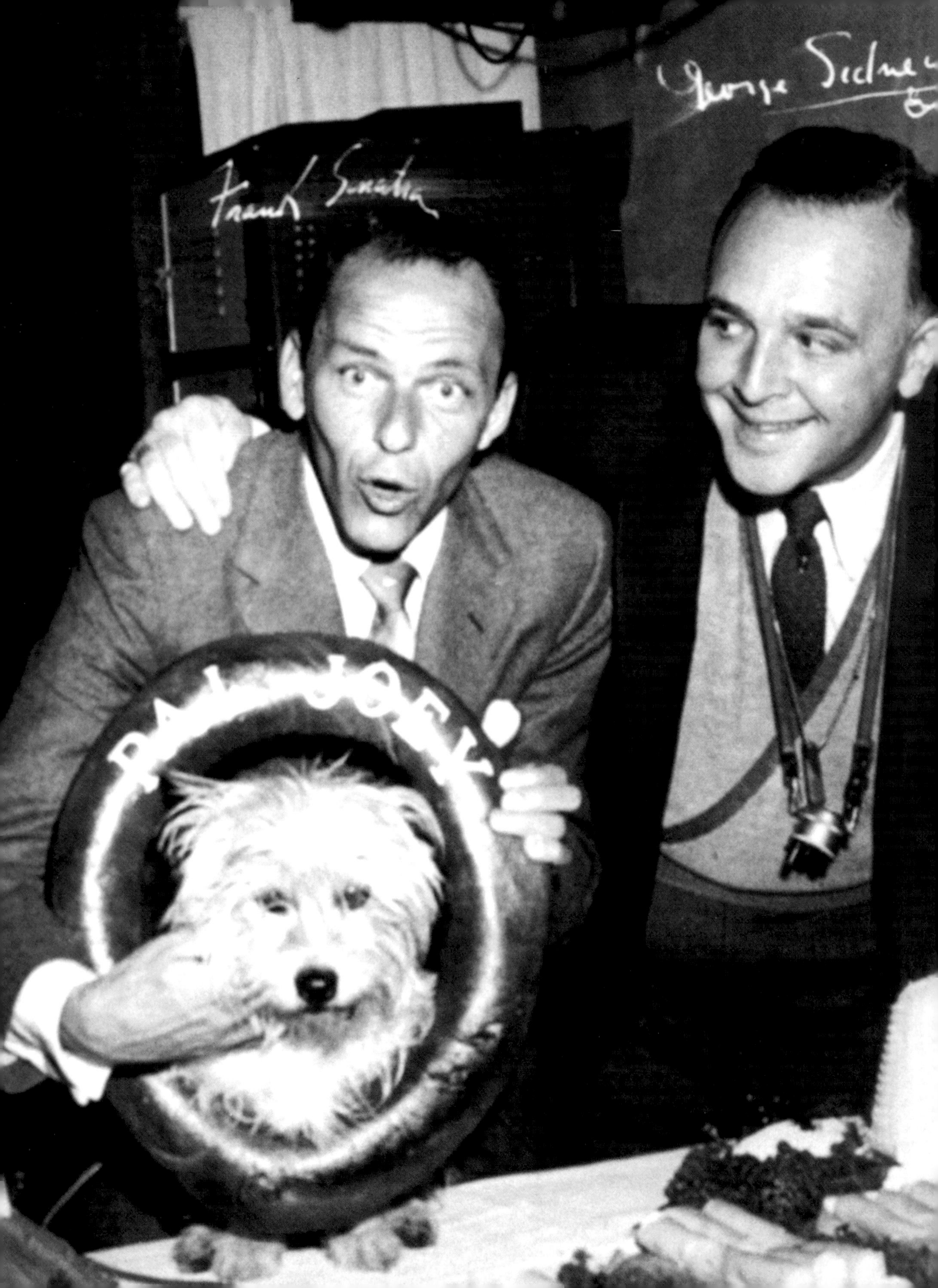
Frank Sinatra
PAL JOEY

THAT'S A WRAP
In Conclusion

When tourists come to New York, the first thing they want to do is to eat — a craving that leads them straight to a deli. People from all walks of life and of all nationalities think of New York food as deli food. The mystique of this simple ethnic menu is as much a part of the New York scene as the Statue of Liberty, the Empire State Building, or a Broadway play. One must try a corned beef or pastrami sandwich with all the trimmings — the pickles, the coleslaw, the soda and then, of course, the cheesecake. No trip to New York would be complete without them. Deli is the true New York eating experience.

There is a richness to this food not only in its tastes, smells, and textures but in the rich history and tradition that it evokes. The savory strudels of Hungary, the pungent borscht from Russia, and the mouthwatering cheesecakes of Eastern Europe began not in America but many years ago in countries other than our own. The history that they carry is a tradition that should be treasured.

The deli culture is slowly diminishing in cities throughout the country, but as people look for solace and a place to gather with friends, the deli is the place that could again restore that sense of community. It is my hope that this cultural history will spark the interest in all things deli so that the delicatessen culture will again be in the forefront of the eating experience across America. And as people long for traditional foods, they will find it in this, the ultimate comfort food.

Page 168: Photo, 1957. Frank Sinatra, director George Sidney, and "pals" celebrate the completion of the movie *Pal Joey* at Nate 'n Al's Delicatessen in Beverly Hills, California. *(Courtesy of Nate 'n Al's Delicatessen)*

Opposite page: Photo, 1927. The exterior of Dave's Delicatessen on Sixth Avenue and Washington Place in New York City. This image shows the prominence of delicatessen life in the early part of the twentieth century. *(Courtesy of The New York Historical Society)*

Acknowledgments

In essence, this book is a scrapbook, and many people helped to make the scrapbook come together.

Thanks go first and foremost to my daughter, Lauren Rott, for her encouragement when I thought my head was going to burst, and for her extensive knowledge of English and Yiddish. Her editing skills were also invaluable. She was an all-around dependable helpmate. Thank you, Lauren!

Thank you, Brian and Debbie, for aiding me through many computer glitches; Allison, for your encouragement; and Joel, for tasting your way through this experience with me.

The recipes and photographs, many of which are lovingly and carefully guarded, are courtesy of museums, delicatessens, and individuals named here, and I thank them. To Gary Canter, Canter's Deli, for plying me with huge platters of food; Mark Canter; Marc Mendelson and Jay Kornblum, Nate 'n Al's; Gary Greengrass, Barney Greengrass; Josh Tupper, Russ & Daughters Appetizing Store; Terry Lebewohl, 2nd Avenue Deli; Steve Auerbach and Jay Heyman, Stage Deli; Sandy Levine, The Carnegie Deli; Roberta Sperling, Ben's Kosher Delicatessen; Kenny Kohn and Lois Kroff, Katz's Deli; Tim Baker, Guss' Lower East Side Pickles; Ari Weitzwig, Zingerman's Delicatessen; Norm Langer, Langer's Deli; Fred Harmatz, Ratner's; Steve Oh, Eisenberg's Sandwich Shop; Dick Werth, Rose's Deli; Irv Schnider and Terry Felper-Giordano; Debbie and Suzee Markowitz, Factor's Famous Deli; Alan Rosen, Junior's; Rita Silverman; Jeffrey Segal, The Riese Organization; Irv Feldman, Olde Tyme Deli; Brian Shapiro and Tracy Fiddler, Shapiro's Delicatessen; Marc Attman, Attman's; David Auspitz, Famous 4th Street Deli; Natalie Brown, Kosher Cajun Deli; Neil Akin, D. Z. Akin's Deli; Earl Stein, Corky & Lenny's; Yonah Schimmel Knishes; Hebrew National; Economy Candy; Danny Raskin, the *Detroit Jewish News*; Mark Gold, Gold's Pure Food Products Co., Inc.; Alan Adler, Streit's Matzo; Karen Weinberg, Empire National Kosher Foods; B. Manischewitz Co., LLC; David and Kelly Fox, Fox's u-bet Syrup; Dr. Brown's Cola; I. Rokeach and Son's; Fleischmann's Yeast; Acme Smoked Fish; Joyva Halvah; Greg McCoy, Proctor & Gamble; Steve Ross, Coney Island Bialy Bakery; Israel Moskowitz, Gertel's Bake Shoppe; Yura Dashevsky; Nathan's Famous, Inc.; Rabbi Peter Schweitzer; Steve Siegel, 92nd Street Y; Stuart Rockhoff, The Museum of the Southern Jewish Experience; Dale Rosengarten, The College of Charleston Jewish Heritage Collection; Jill Reichenbach, The New York Historical Society; and Nora Galler, The Georgia Historical Society.

INDEX

INDEX

Photo, 2005. Éclairs and Napoleons found in the famous pastry case at Rose's Deli in Portland, Oregon.
(Courtesy of Rose's Deli)

INDEX

Photo, 2005 *(Courtesy of Rose's Deli)*

INDEX